THE LOVE MYTH

THE LOVE MYTH

EXPLORING THE MYTH OF
"FALLING IN LOVE"
AS THE BASIS FOR A
SUCCESSFUL MARRIAGE.

GODWIN UDE

WinePress Publishing
Great Books, Defined.

WinePress Publishing is honored to present this title in partnership with the author. The views expressed or implied in this work are those of the author. WinePress provides our imprint seal representing design excellence, creative content and high quality production. To learn more about Responsible Publishing™ visit www.winepresspublishing.com.

ISBN 13: 978-1-4141-2512-1
ISBN 10: 1-4141-2512-7
Library of Congress Catalog Card Number: 2012919402

CONTENTS

CHAPTER 1

SNOW WHITE SAID SO

Some day my prince will come; some day we'll meet again
And away to his castle we'll go to be happy forever I know
Some day when spring is here we'll find our love anew
And the birds will sing and wedding bells will ring
Some day when my dreams come true

Snow White, in *Snow White and the Seven Dwarfs*[1]

In 1937, audiences were introduced to *Snow White and the Seven Dwarfs*, the first of fifty-one full-length animated films released by Walt Disney Productions.[2] The movie begins with Snow White, a princess, living with her wicked stepmother, the queen. Each day, the queen gazes into her magic mirror and asks, "Magic mirror on the wall, who is the fairest one of all?" As long as the mirror answers, "You are the fairest one of all," Snow White is safe from the queen's jealousy.

But the day comes when the mirror answers, "Famed is thy beauty, Majesty. But hold, a lovely maid I see.... Alas, she is more fair than thee." Enraged, the queen orders her huntsman to take Snow White into the woods and kill her. The huntsman reluctantly agrees, but when he lifts the knife to slay her, he finds he cannot do it. So instead, he tells the princess about the plot and urges her to run away.

Snow White flees into the forest until she finds a cottage inhabited by seven dwarfs. When the dwarfs realize that she can cook, clean, and keep up the house, they invite her to stay. It is here in the cottage that Snow White sings the wistful song "Some Day My Prince Will Come" as a bedtime lullaby for the dwarfs.

The queen soon discovers that she has been tricked. This time, she decides to take matters into her own hands. She disguises herself as an old hag and creates a poisoned apple that will put Snow White into a "sleeping death." When the dwarfs are away, the queen visits the cottage and convinces Snow White to eat the apple. The princess immediately falls into a deep slumber.

When the dwarfs return home, they find Snow White's lifeless body and believe she is dead. They place her in a glass coffin, which they set in a clearing in the woods. After some time, a prince (who had previously fallen in love with Snow White) comes along and discovers her. He is saddened by her death and kisses her. The power of true love's kiss breaks the spell, and Snow White awakens. The prince takes Snow White to his castle, which glows in her presence, and the two live happily ever after.

A Common Theme

Snow White—and many other children's films that have followed over the years—carry a common theme: love, falling in love, or finding one's true love. The message in each of these films seems to be the same: there is someone out there just waiting for you, and when you find that person you will instantly fall in love and live together happily for the rest of your lives. While it is odd that this theme would be prevalent in movies made for children—who have a number of years to go before they even reach pubescence, much less an age where they can understand the emotional rollercoaster of being "in love"—filmmakers have made a killing turning out these types of films. Consider this love song sung by the lead character in *Sleeping Beauty*, a children's classic released by Disney in 1959:

I know you
I walked with you once upon a dream
I know you
The gleam in your eyes is so familiar a gleam
Yes, I know it's true
That visions are seldom all they seem
But if I know you, I know what you'll do
You'll love me at once
The way you did once upon a dream.[3]

Three generations later, in the film *Pocahontas*, John Smith and Pocahontas sang lyrics that showed the theme of emotional love was as strong as ever:

If I never knew you
If I never felt this love
I would have no inkling of
How precious life can be
And if I never held you
I would never have a clue
How at last I'd find in you
The missing part of me.[4]

In truth, our first experience or view of love typically comes through the lens of multimedia—often through these children's classics. As we grow older, the Disney movies of our childhood give way to romantic comedies such as *Clueless, Enchanted*, and *The Princess Diaries* and to romantic dramas such as *Twilight*, which received this review on the KidsWorld website:

> Life sucks when your soul mate is a hundred-year-old vampire who has to resist the urge to literally eat you up. Considering the age gap and diet differences, Edward and Bella manage to do all right with the whole doomed lovers deal—sure there's pining and wistful sighs, but those dramatics are part of the reason *Twilight* has staked the number one spot in so many hearts.[5]

Not only do we find this theme in movies and on television, but we also get a healthy dose of it in our popular music. Love songs blare over the radio as we drive, and we sing along at the top of our lungs to lyrics such as these:

> *I want to be the face you see when you close your eyes*
> *I want to be the touch you need every single night*
> *I want to be your fantasy and be your reality and everything between*
> *I want you to need me like the air you breathe.*[6]

Steamy romance novels wait upon our bedside tables for the moments we can't sleep, compelling us to buy into this idea of true love. And if we're not avid readers, we have other ways of receiving this message in our technological age, such as interactive role-playing video games and matchmaking sites that offer casual encounters, where the only limit is one's imagination.

Arranged Marriages

It's not only the Western hemisphere that seems fixated on the feeling of being in love. In India, the film *Love Aaj Kal* ("Love

These Days") was declared a "super hit" by *Box Office India*, grossing $16.2 million during its run.[7] The film portrayed the message that as long as two people are in love, nothing else really matters—a theme that is unique in a nation where parents and relatives still play a major part in the decision-making process of marriage.

In India, when a son or daughter is deemed old enough to marry, a parent or other relative acts as a sponsor to find a suitable candidate for the young person to marry. The sponsor typically works through a matchmaker—often an elderly socialite connected to many families—to find a suitable candidate who meets both the young person's and the family's criteria. While these criteria vary, they often include religion, caste, horoscope (numerology and the position of the stars are believed to predict the success of the match), profession, status, and physical appearance. Once the matchmaker finds a candidate who fulfills the criteria, photos and information are exchanged and an interview is set up. If there is interest from both sides—and no red flags—the engagement is announced.

Although this idea of arranged marriages might sound odd to us, if not completely disagreeable, the truth is that this is just the way it was throughout a majority of recorded history. In times past, arranged marriages were the primary method for matching life partners, not only in the Middle East and Far East—as portrayed in the Old Testament story of Abraham finding a wife for his son Isaac (see Gen. 24)—but in Europe as well. In fact, throughout the Middle Ages the parents usually chose the partner for their sons and daughters. This practice continued well into the nineteenth century.

In royal families, marriages were seen as a way to unite families, keep royal bloodlines pure, and develop one's empire. Young brides were viewed as currency and items of exchange more than anything else. This is not to say that the young bride and groom were always opposed to the match or forced together, although doubtless at times that did happen. Rather, matrimony was viewed differently than it is today, for couples did not have the same romantic notions of marriage that we have now.

Of course, in our modern era, both prospective partners have a say in the match. Even in countries such as India, the practice of arranged marriages is waning in the face of the media's celebration of romantic love. However, whether the marriage is arranged or not, it still must consist of more than just the feelings of love the partners share.

The Problem of Romanticism

In Europe, the shift from arranged marriages to being in love as the most important factor in deciding a relationship occurred during the late eighteenth century. As the people of that era grew tired of what they viewed as the cold rationalism of the Age of Enlightenment and the stuffy traditions of the upper classes, they looked for a more idealized view of marriage and relationships. The result was Romanticism, which the *Encyclopedia Britannica* defines this way:

> [An] attitude or intellectual orientation that characterized many works of literature, painting, music, architecture, criticism, and historiography in Western civilization over a period from the late 18th to the mid-19th century.... Romanticism emphasized the individual, the subjective, the irrational, the imaginative, the personal, the spontaneous, the emotional, the visionary, and the transcendental. Among the characteristic attitudes of Romanticism were ... a general exaltation of emotion over reason and of the senses over intellect; a turning in upon the self and a heightened examination of human personality and its moods and mental potentialities ... [and] a focus on passions and inner struggles.[8]

As C.S. Lewis notes in his book *The Four Loves*, Romanticism brought "'tearful comedy' and the 'return to nature' and the exaltation of Sentiment; and in their train all that great wallow of emotion which, though often criticized, has lasted ever since."[9]

Of course, this is not to say there is anything inherently wrong with emotions and romance. Without the splashes of color that emotion brings to our lives, we would exist in a world of dreary shades of gray. Likewise, without romance, we wouldn't have the candlelight dinners we all dream about, complete with flowers, wine, and moonlit walks along the beach with that special someone.

The difficulty lies in the focus that has been placed on being in love to the exclusion of all the other factors that make up a relationship. If we base our decisions solely on what we read in romance novels, see in movies, or hear in the music around us, we will be led to believe that falling in love is the single most important thing to consider when deciding on a relationship or life partner.

But where will that leave us when the happily-ever-after we have been promised suddenly eludes our grasp? What happens when the rosy glow fades, the reality of life kicks in, and the knight and maiden in a magical castle morph into a normal husband and wife who need to pay the bills, clean the house, and raise the kids? What do we do when emotions fade and those dreamy and delightful feelings give way to familiarity and criticism? What do we do if—heaven forbid—those passionate emotions begin to rise for someone other than our significant partner?

If we have bought into the world's concept of true love, we will have no option but to end the relationship. After all, something must be terribly wrong if we no longer have the feelings we once did when we sang those old love songs, like this one:

My love, here I stand before you
I am yours now from this moment on
Take my hand, only you can stop me shaking
We'll share forever, this I promise you ...
As we dance now closer than before
Don't let go, 'cause I could almost cry now
This is forever, I make this vow to you
My darling, this I promise you.[10]

What happened to love's eternal promise? If those in-love feelings are no longer enough to create a wonderful and lasting relationship, what is? It can't be reason; that would be too calculating. It can't be practicality; that would be too self-serving. After all, isn't love the most important thing, the "greatest of these" (1 Cor. 13:13)?

What Is Love?

Although the distinction is not often made, there are different forms of that state we call love. In fact, many languages have a number of different words to describe these varied states. The ancient Greeks, for example, had at least four words for the concept of love, ranging from godly love to simple affection. Today, Hindi has at least five words for love, and Japanese has at least six. In English, however, we have only one word for this vastly multifaceted emotion.

But is *emotion* truly the best word to describe love? Are there other words that more accurately portray and manifest what love truly is? Could love more aptly be termed an action—*what we do* rather than *how we feel*? If we were to change our perception of love and make that distinction between emotion and action, we might find that love is something deeper and greater than we had ever hoped and dreamed, and within that discovery find the power to love and be loved in return.

CHAPTER 2

THE SOUL MATE DECEPTION

Is that a kind of occupational hazard of soul mates—one's not much without the other?

Robin Williams, in *What Dreams May Come*[11]

A true love that transcends the difficulties of life, overcomes death's great divide, reaches down into hell itself, and brings two people together in heavenly bliss ... the story line seems as if it could come straight from the Bible, but it's actually from the novel *What Dreams May Come,* written in 1978 by Richard Matheson. Made into a major motion picture starring Robin Williams, Cuba Gooding Jr., and Annabella Sciorra, it is just one of many books and movies that deal with the subject of finding one's soul mate.

In the story, a physician named Chris Nielsen (played by Robin Williams) meets an artist (played by Annabella Sciorra) while vacationing in Switzerland. The two are immediately attracted to one another—almost as if they had known each other for a long time before—and they marry and have a family. After experiencing a horrible tragedy, the two almost separate, but they manage to stay together. Then, on the anniversary of the day they decided not to divorce, Chris is killed in a car crash.

He goes to heaven, where he finds that the landscape is controlled by his thoughts. He soon meets a man named Albert (played by Cuba Gooding Jr.), who serves as his guide and teaches him how to shape his surroundings. At one point, a blue jacaranda tree appears unbidden onto the scene, which Chris realizes is from a painting his wife was drawing after his death. He marvels that the tree could be present in heaven. "It's completely new," he says to Albert. "The canvas was blank when I was alive. How can I see this drawing after I'm dead?"

"Did you and Annie have a long courtship?" Albert asks.

"No, actually," Chris replies, "from the very first moment it was like—"

"Soul mates," Albert says, completing his sentence. "It's extremely rare but it exists. Sort of like twin souls tuned into each other. Apparently, even in death."

This idea of two people sharing a twin soul is woven into the plots of many other movies. In *City of Angels* (1998), an angel is willing to live a mortal life on earth just to be with his soul mate. In *Serendipity* (2001), a man and woman spend just one day together, but they are so sure they are made for each other that they end up spending five years trying to reconnect (fate ultimately brings them together). In *August Rush* (2007), a man and woman spend a single *night* together, but both find they cannot forget the other. For more than a decade, they live separate lives, but eventually fate intervenes and brings them back together. They are soul mates, after all, and they are meant to be.

The idea that each of us has a soul mate—a person who will complete us—is certainly compelling. But where does it leave those of us who have not yet found our other half? Most likely, we will find ourselves believing that the one with whom we were meant to spend the rest of our lives is still out there ... somewhere. So the search begins. At a Starbucks. On a train. In a high school cafeteria or a church fellowship hall. Our eyes and hearts are open—and often our arms as well.

The Origin of the Concept

Where did this notion of soul mate come from, and how accurate (or inaccurate) is it? Some believe it originated with the Greek belief that when the god Zeus created humans, he split the soul in two before sending it to earth—male and female halves of one perfect soul. If those two found each other, they could be complete and spend the rest of their lives in passion's bliss. Others attribute the idea to Plato. In his writings in *The Symposium*, he states that Zeus originally created humans with four arms, four legs, and a single head made of two faces, but after creating humans Zeus began to fear their power, so he split them into two. As a result, humans spend eternity searching for their other half so they can be complete.

Still others point to the Bible as the origin of the idea. In the book of Genesis, when God created Adam and placed him in the garden of Eden, He said, "It is not good that man should be alone; I will make him a helper comparable to him" (Gen. 2:18). God put Adam into a deep sleep, took one of his ribs, formed Eve, and brought her to the man. Many believe that because God created Eve for Adam in this manner, it only makes sense that He would do the same for people today. Furthermore, if God has a particular destiny (or "predestination") for each of His children, it would only stand to reason that He would have the perfect individual in mind for each of them as well.

This idea seems to be validated when that chance meeting does take place—let's say at a college graduation party of a mutual acquaintance—and two people find they are immediately and mutually attracted to one another. Perhaps they schedule a second meeting, and a flame of romance begins to kindle. Over time, the couple learns they have many common interests (or maybe just one or two), which pours fuel onto passion's fire. As time goes on and they find they share even more personal likes and dislikes, they begin to believe even more strongly in what every steamy novel and romantic comedy has taught them: that two people *can* be made for one another.

The problem with this idea is that *every* person we encounter can represent a unique and special experience—an adventure in growth and learning. We may find we share much in common with these people and yet not have any in-love feelings for them. There are many people in our lives who help us grow and develop, but we would never view them as soul mates who complete us.

The Desire to Belong

Why is this idea of having a soul mate so compelling? One reason is the desire to *belong* built deep within every human being. As children, we begin our lives by belonging to a family unit. The connections we form within our family in our early years vitally affect our development. When that family unit is dysfunctional or lacking, it can lead to us developing neurotic or pathological issues.

As we grow, our need to belong remains every bit as strong, though we begin to fill that need in places outside the home. This is the time when parents hope their children will hang out with a good crowd and find the right friends, because they know (probably from their own experiences during their teen years) that peer pressure is a very real thing. Cliques, groups, and gangs can lead a young person toward a life of purpose and potential or the exact opposite. For many, associating with *any* group of people—even if it is obvious that the group doesn't have a positive effect—is better than remaining alone.

This innate need to belong is what makes the idea of a soul mate so promising. It's beautiful. It's magical. It's just the way things should be. It offers us the hope that if we can just find that one individual in the whole wide world who will complete us and always be with us, we will lead a truly happy and fulfilled life. Rather than facing life alone, we will have someone to walk along that path with us.

When we do meet that person we think is the one, we're suddenly on top of the world. As we stand there hand in hand, it seems there is nothing we cannot do or face together. "Love is all we need" becomes our motto, and it oozes from every pore, in every glance, in every touch. The future is bright. We picture ourselves taking romantic walks on moonlit beaches, with gentle ocean waves rolling along the shore and perpetual background music filling the starry night. It seems that forever is not enough time to discover the other person. We want to share every moment with him or her, know every dream, and fulfill every wish.

Before long, this amazing discovery of our soul mate leads to its natural result: marriage or some other strong commitment. But both partners soon come to realize that not every day is sunny. A misunderstanding or argument breaks out, and the clouds begin to roll in. One partner begins to pull back, and the nights no longer seem to be as starry as we once hoped. Sometimes the mist is so thick we can't see even a single guiding star in the foreboding darkness.

Soon the realization dawns that perhaps the other person isn't our soul mate after all. Tears are shed, promises are broken, the relationship is severed, and the marriage is ended. *I'll be more careful next time*, we promise ourselves as we venture out into the world again. Once more, we find ourselves alone … until the next chance meeting, the next flare of excitement and passion, the next discovery. At last, we feel we have found our *true* soul mate, and the cycle begins once more.

Do Soul Mates Exist?

Is there such a thing as a soul mate? Yes, there is. However, a soul mate is not something that is *discovered*, like a pot of gold at the end of the rainbow, but something that is *made* and built over time. While today the popular idea behind a soul mate gives the impression that the participants do not change and grow as they move through life—that each soul mate is and always will be the perfect person for the other—the truth is that this relationship is not a static state of being. A healthy couple in a *real* relationship continually learns, changes, accommodates, and grows… together.

This may sound like a lot of work, and it is. But where did we get the idea that a relationship should not involve work? Where did we get the notion that a relationship is only ideal if there is nothing but perpetual bliss? How would our world survive without any rain, regardless of how harsh the storms may be at times? Sun and rain, day and night, cloud and clear—all are needed to create the beautiful world in which we live. Trials and triumphs, challenges and blessings, difficulties and victories are all needed to create a soft heart and a strong spirit.

In this life, nothing is perfect, flawless, or without blemish. In fact, it is the imperfections that allow us to appreciate the beauty and uniqueness in each person. If a relationship had no challenges, there would be no opportunity for those in it to develop gifts such as forgiveness, patience, gentleness, and forbearance.

Of course, it is not wrong to search for the right person. No one would ever advocate just picking someone up off the street and heading to the nearest city hall to tie the knot. We must use wisdom, discretion, discernment, and counsel in the process of finding a life partner. The bottom line, however, is that we will never find the *perfect* soul mate, nor will we be the perfect soul mate for someone else. It is only through loving, dedication, and prayer that life partners develop and share a deep connection in their souls. In the end, a relationship is what the partners make it.

In the Bible, God compares our relationship with Christ—the greatest relationship possible—to that of a husband and wife (see Eph. 5:22–23). This should provide us with a hint that it is not only possible for a marriage to be enduring, but it is also possible for a marriage to be deep. Our relationship with our spouse is meant to be a long-term uniting of souls rather than a quick discovery of a twin soul. For this reason, if two people decide to commit to a life together and share the vows of marriage, those two are "the one" for each other. Neither can claim their spouse wasn't their soul mate and that the right one must be out there somewhere. There might be some who represent a better fit for one another, but there is no perfect relationship, because there are no perfect people.

Remember that Jesus came into this world to save every imperfect being on this earth, and He calls those who accept His love His bride (Rev. 21:9). He loved each of us so much—even with our imperfections—that He gave up His very life so that we would not perish but would have eternal life (see John 3:16). This is the kind of love we must strive to manifest to others—including our significant other.

CHAPTER 3

THE REAL WORLD

In every marriage more than a week old, there are grounds for divorce. The trick is to find and continue to find grounds for marriage.

Robert Anderson

It is not easy to accept that the happily-ever-after world of Disney is just a fairy tale and the perfect soul mate just doesn't exist. Each of us wants the stories of eternally blissful relationships we read about in books and see in the movies to be true. Looking at the true state of the world around us is depressing, especially when we consider just how many marriages end in divorce.

When two people are caught up in the embrace of passionate love and are considering taking the next step of commitment, the last thing they want to think about is divorce. No one experiencing the highs of being in love ever believes such a thing could happen to them—they assume that divorce only happens to other couples. Yet the sad fact is that a high number of marriages worldwide *do* end in divorce, and the percentage only continues to grow each year.

Some believe the solution to the problem is cohabitation, or living together without being married, but statistics do not seem to support this conclusion. In a 2002 study conducted by the Centers for Disease Control and Prevention, researchers actually found that cohabitations are *less stable* than marriages. While 20 percent of couples in a first marriage were likely to end up separated or divorced within the first five years, *49 percent* of cohabiting couples were likely to break up within the same time frame. After ten years, the probability of a first marriage ending jumps to 33 percent, while the probability for cohabitations ending jumps to *62 percent.*[12]

These findings are not unique to the United States. In a government report conducted by the Australian Institute of Family Studies, researchers found that "regardless of the period in which cohabitation or marriage began, the likelihood of a cohabiting relationship ending in separation within 5 years was 3 to 5 times the likelihood of a marriage ending in divorce within 5 years (25 to 38 percent versus 7 to 9 percent)."[13] In light of these findings, it is clear that choosing to avoid marriage as a means of keeping a relationship together is not a viable option.

Divorce Rates Worldwide

To determine just how bad the problem has become, we need to examine and analyze some of the data that has been collected on divorce rates worldwide. As you read these statistics, note that the ratio of marriages to divorces (for the most part) relates to a particular year. For example, a divorce rate of 50 percent for 2010 would signify that for every one hundred thousand people who married that year, fifty thousand ended up getting a divorce. When I compare the number of divorces to the actual number of marriages, I cite the statistics a bit differently—for example, I might state that in 2010 there were 11.5 divorces for every thousand marriages across England. In other words, the percentages indicate the ratio of marriages to divorces for a particular year, rather than the ratio of total married couples to the number of divorces for that year.[14]

Divorce Rate in the United States

A commonly held belief is that 50 percent of all marriages in the United States end in divorce. Although this statement is not entirely correct, the truth is that if the current trend continues, 50 percent of all marriages in the United States *will* end up this way. Thirty years ago, only 35 in one thousand marriages in America ended in divorce, but by 1993 that figure had quadrupled to 148 in one thousand marriages, and by 1999 it had reached 240 in one thousand marriages.[15] Thus, the statement that 50 percent of marriages in the United States end in divorce is more of a projection.

The ratio of divorces to marriages in America is actually skewed a bit, because studies show that the more times a person marries after a divorce, the more likely he or she is to divorce again. According to an article published in *Enrichment Journal*, 41 percent of first marriages, 60 percent of second marriages, and 73 percent of third marriages fail.

Among women, those in the age range of 20–24 are the most likely to divorce (36.6 percent)—possibly because they are also the most likely to marry—followed by those under 20 years old (27.6 percent). Among men, those in the age range of 20–24 have highest rate of divorce (38.8 percent), followed by those in the age range of 25–29 (22.3 percent). One interesting fact is that couples without children have a higher divorce rate than couples who are raising children.

Divorce Rate in Canada

According to a report compiled by the Department of Justice in 1997, the divorce rate in Canada stands at approximately 48 percent. Again, subsequent marriages are more likely to end in divorce, with a probability of 72 percent of second marriages failing and a probability of 85 percent of third marriages failing.

More recent statistics published in an article by CBC News show that approximately four in ten first marriages in Canada will end in divorce. The article goes on to state that according to Statistics Canada, about 38 percent of all marriages taking place in 2004 will have ended in divorce by 2035. In addition, while the total divorce rate in Canada has decreased slightly from its peak of about 41 percent in the mid 1980s, today it is slightly higher than the rate of about 37 percent that was recorded in the mid 1990s. [16]

Divorce Rate in the United Kingdom

According to data published by the Office for National Statistics, in 2010 the divorce rate in England and Wales rose for the first time in seven years, with 119,589 couples choosing to end their marriages. As an article in *The Guardian* states, "The numbers of people divorcing are the equivalent of one couple parting for every two that marry each year. The figure equates to 11.1 per 1,000 married people—up from 10.5 in 2009."[17] Men and women in their late twenties constituted the highest divorce rates per age bracket. In Northern Ireland and Scotland, the divorce rate in 2008 decreased approximately 5 percent from the previous year, with the proportion of people who had already gone through one or more divorces being far greater (the figure has doubled since 1981).[18]

Divorce Rate in Australia

According to the Australian Bureau of Statistics, in 2010 approximately 41 percent of marriages in Australia ended in divorce.[19] This represented a 1 percent increase over the previous year, and the number of divorces has been steadily climbing over the past few years.

Divorce Rate in Japan

The divorce rate in Japan is roughly half that found in North America and Europe, with one in every four marriages ending in divorce. As of the most recent study, Japan's divorce rate is roughly 27 percent.

Divorce Rate in India

India has one of the lowest divorce rates in the world, with only 1.1 percent of marriages ending in divorce. However, this figure is actually up from 1990, when the divorce rate stood at approximately .07 percent. In addition, it is interesting to note that the divorce rate in villages is remarkably lower than in cities and urban areas—a fact that gives credence to the idea that the effects of modern life and media play a large part in perceptions of love, relationships, marriage, and divorce.

Effects of Divorce

With divorces being so common today, it is easy to become desensitized to the problem and neglect to look at the realities of what divorce means for those who go through it—especially when children are involved. In *A Long Way East of Eden*, author Pete Lowman cites the following statistics that reveal just how deeply divorce affects families:

- Those who are divorced or separated are four times more likely to need psychiatric help than those who are married.
- Married people find it easier to adjust to illness or disability than those who do not have a life partner.
- Children of divorced parents find it significantly more difficult as adults to develop a lasting relationship with a partner.
- Children from broken homes are significantly more likely to suffer from mental disturbances.
- Children of divorced parents tend to be more economically and socially disadvantaged as compared to children of married parents.
- Suicide rates are higher in divorced families, with 86 percent of teenage suicides occurring in fatherless families.
- Sexual abuse is much more common in families without two natural parents.
- Of fathers who have been found to sexually abuse their children, more than 60 percent had parents who were divorced.[20]

Other studies show that children ages 3–5 years will frequently believe they caused their parents' divorce and will fear being left alone or abandoned. Elementary school–aged children, who are particularly hard-hit by divorce, are more likely to experience bouts of grief, embarrassment, resentment, and intense anger. Adolescents and teens will experience anger, fear, loneliness, depression, and guilt, and many will feel pressured into adulthood when faced with additional chores and taking care of younger siblings. Those in this age group may begin to doubt their own ability to get married or to stay married.[21]

Reasons for Divorce

Considering the damaging and long-term effects of these breakups, one may wonder why society at large has such a flippant view of divorce. One reason may be that people simply do not understand the harmful effects of divorce on families. In a world where divorce rates top out at 50 percent, it is easy to rationalize that it is no big deal and that "the kids will get through it." Another likely reason is that people have bought into the idea that once couples realize they are incompatible, it is better for them to separate than stay miserable. "They've fallen out of love, and you can't expect them to stay together when they're no longer in love."

With the huge number of divorces and separations occurring worldwide, individual cases rarely hit the news. When they do, it is usually apparent that what one person (or both) in the relationship considers to be love has played a large part in the dissolution of the marriage. Consider, for example, the strange case of a forty-one-year-old teacher named James Hooker, who in February 2012 left his wife and children to pursue a relationship with an eighteen-year-old student. The effects of Hooker's actions on his family were devastating, as the family's pastor related in a statement to the *Modesto Bee:* "This is a very difficult time for them, so family, friends and the church body have gathered around to support them as they work through the pain caused by James' decision to abandon his family."[22]

Hooker himself admitted that he had caused his family great pain. "In making our choice, we've hurt a lot of people," he said in an interview with the *Modesto Bee.* "We keep asking ourselves, 'Do we make everyone else happy or do we follow our hearts?'"[23] Hooker's statement sounds almost noble, as if he and his eighteen-year-old love interest, united in love, are standing alone against the rest of the world for the cause of following one's heart. However, in the words of C.S. Lewis,

> When lovers say of some act that we might blame, "Love made us do it," notice ... how tremulously, almost how devoutly, they say the word love, not so much pleading an extenuating circumstance as appealing to an authority.... "In love," we have our own "law," a religion of our own, our own god.... It seems to sanction all sorts of actions they would not otherwise have dared. The pair can say to one another in an almost sacrificial spirit, "It is for love's sake that I have neglected my parents—left my children—cheated my partner—failed my friend at his greatest need." These reasons in love's law have passed for good.[24]

As a reporter for the *San Francisco Weekly* acutely summed up, Hooker was clearly "blinded by love."[25] But is *love* the word that accurately describes what was happening in this situation? Was Hooker truly following his heart, or has the word *love*—and all that it should stand for—been tainted through wrongful actions sanctioned by those in the throes of passion? Do such actions as a man leaving his wife and children deserve to be classified as love? We will take a closer look at this in the next chapter.

CHAPTER 4

LOVE OR LIMERENCE?

Lay a whisper on my pillow, leave the winter on the ground.
I wake up lonely, there's air of silence in the bedroom and all around.
Touch me now, I close my eyes and dream away …
It must have been love, but it's over now.

Per Gessle, from "It Must Have Been Love"[26]

This song, recorded by the band Roxette in the 1980s, describes a particular in-love state that scientist Dorothy Tennov called *limerence*. According to Dr. Tennov,

> Limerence is an identifiable and invariant condition that afflicts persons identically whenever it occurs and is mainly characterized by a unique form of cognitive preoccupation. The condition is commonly referred to as "being in love," "romantic love," or "passionate love." …

> Limerence can and often does exist apart from an overt relationship between the limerent person and the person who is the object of limerence (LO).... Limerence reorders the motivational hierarchy, with the consequent disruption or neglect of other interests, relationships, and responsibilities. Limerence can occur at any adult age and tends to be long-lasting once it takes hold....
>
> Limerence intensity is a function of interpretations of the behavior of its [limerent] object (LO) regarding probability of "reciprocation." Reciprocation is that behavior of LO which is interpretable by the limerent person as indicating a similar yearning for merger in a committed and "mutually loving" relationship. There is only one LO (at a time)....
>
> [The limerent person's] mood depends on hope—the limerent person may walk on air when expectations are positive, but feel deep despair at rejection.... To those in its grip, it is an essential ingredient of a satisfying life. [In their perception], anyone not limerent is missing something important. Conversely, those who have not experienced limerence find it difficult to imagine....
>
> The course of limerence is dictated by interpretation of LO's feelings. At the outset, limerence is felt to be merely pleasurable attraction. Given the proper ingredients of hope and uncertainty, it progresses rapidly.... Events dictate both its intensity and whether the experience is painful or pleasurable....
>
> The main danger [of limerence] is the failure [of those involved] to give appropriate attention to other aspects of life.[27]

Dr. Tennov, who conducted her research during the 1970s, began her work out of a desire to study the common occurrence among couples of being in love. She had found that psychologists made no distinction between in-love feelings and other forms of love, and her goal was to show, in part, that this state of being—which she called limerence—was not real love. Her findings revealed that while certain aspects of limerence and love are similar, in other ways they are worlds apart.

Characteristics of Limerence

An informative article by Joe Beam, a Christian marriage counselor and chairman of the Beam Research Center, sheds more light on the physiological effects of limerence:

> In this state the limerent's brain increases dopamine (the ecstasy, happy, feel-good chemical in the brain) and decreases serotonin (the inhibitor, finish things, bring things to a conclusion chemical in the brain). To draw us toward the lover and overcome any barriers that might distract or prohibit us from pursuing, the brain goes into a phase in which logic and intelligence surrender to feelings and emotions. It's a natural high that is as strong, if not stronger, than nearly any drug. And it gets stronger.
>
> Emotions continue to intensify as fear develops that somehow one may lose the LO and the relationship will not last. Fear increases passion. That's why it is so euphoric while at the same time so scary. In short, the limerent's brain is a cauldron of unbalanced chemicals that lead to the absolute misery of blissfully intense love; happy thoughts mixed with fearful thoughts, wonderful fantasies about the future diluted by nagging doubts, euphoria sometimes dropping suddenly into depression, and giddiness competing with Godliness.[28]

According to Dr. Beam, limerence is not infatuation (which is also known as having a crush on someone) but a state in which a person is "madly and overwhelmingly in love to the point of obsession."[29] While the focus of an infatuation can be an ideal, a hero, or an object, limerence is exclusively sexual in nature and only extended to a member of the preferred gender. In addition, while infatuation in an individual is generally overwhelming but short-lived, limerence is a long-term state—occasionally lasting up to nine years—yet *invariably it comes to an end*. When it does, the person who was in limerence often finds that his or her perception of the limerent object has changed dramatically. As Dr. Tennov noted, "When limerence has ended, the formerly most-important person may not even be liked. The recovered limerent might feel utterly ashamed and embarrassed about the former obsession."[30]

A distinguishing characteristic of those in limerence is that they have an extreme preoccupation and yearning for the object of their desire to reciprocate their feelings—and they often do not take into account any possibilities other than the eventual realization of their intended outcome. While true love involves concern for the overall well-being of the other person and continues to give regardless of whether it stands to gain from the act, limerence is completely self-centered. Dr. M. Scott Peck describes this aspect of limerence in his book *The Road Less Traveled*:

> Of all the misconceptions about love, the most powerful and pervasive is the belief that "falling in love" is love or at least one of the manifestations of love. It is a potent misconception, because falling in love is subjectively experienced in a very powerful fashion as an experience of love.... Two problems are immediately apparent. The first is that the experience of falling in love is specifically a sex-linked erotic experience.... The second problem is that the experience of falling in love is invariably temporary.[31]

Some scientists and psychologists maintain that these in-love feelings are a necessary function of the human body. They state that if these feelings did not develop so strongly, there would be nothing to compel people to break down the walls they build up to keep themselves safe. In other words, there would be no motivation for anyone to risk reaching out to others in a way that might lead to rejection, hurt, humiliation, or loss. The overwhelming feelings of limerence cause individuals to overcome these fears and hesitations.

The Power of Limerence

This raises the question as to whether we have any control over these types of feelings. According to Dr. Tennov, limerence is an involuntary state in which we have "a totally engaging inability to get the loved one and desire for response from that person out of [our] mind or out of [our] system. [It is] an involuntary affliction that, once it takes hold, is a constant, intrusive, invisible companion [until the state of limerence fades or is transferred]."[32]

However, this does not mean that when we are affected by limerence we have no choice but to accept the emotional roller coaster for as long as it chooses to remain. As Dr. Beam writes, "Just as God heals some naturally and some supernaturally from their physical diseases, He can and will heal them either naturally or supernaturally from their 'brain' and emotional misdirections such as limerence. The primary difference is that they have to yield to Him rather than to their flesh."[33]

Again, the state of being in love is not always a misdirection or something negative. If two people fall in love and decide to pursue a lasting relationship, it is unlikely anyone would step up and say, "You cannot get together, because being in love is a sign that two people are not right for each other." The problem arises when two people use limerence, the *state* of being in love—as their only reason for being together. The idea that love is all we need will not hold up in a marriage relationship. Over time, the strong feelings will eventually fade, and if that is all the marriage or relationship is built on, it will crumble.

In the same way, individuals who are already married or in committed relationships must be careful about the feelings they allow to grow in their hearts. Just as in the example of James Hooker in the previous chapter, who left his wife and children to pursue a relationship with a young student, someone in an in-love state can easily make decisions based on emotion rather than reason. After all, a new love can seem exciting, interesting, and fun, especially when compared to the normal and even boring life we may have been leading for years. In addition, when some new acquaintance shows interest, it's tempting for us to want to return the favor (particularly if it's already been on our minds). We suddenly see with new eyes, the world takes on a rosy glow, we feel warm and fuzzy inside, and we can't help but do something about it.

Unfortunately, all too often we *do* choose to do something about it, which leads to breakups and the divorce epidemic we are witnessing worldwide.

Is Love Doomed to Die?

At this point, you might be saying, "Hold on a minute. I've been told that being in love is nothing but a chemical imbalance—an overdose of dopamine and a reduction in serotonin—and that it's going to fade. If what you are saying is true, what hope is there for me to have a lasting relationship or an enduring marriage? Is love doomed?"

Once again, it is important to remember that limerence, or "being in love," is different from love itself. It is unfortunate that this overwhelming emotion has been pushed to the forefront and all the other forms of love have been relegated to the back burner (which is switched off!). Limerence has been promoted and glorified in the media to the detriment of relationships everywhere.

Fortunately, there is a way to distinguish between these different forms of love. We are not doomed to a permanent guessing game in which we have to continually try to discern exactly what true love means. There are some concrete definitions and expressions of love, and understanding these different forms of this complex term can enable us to live a life filled with love—a *true love* that endures.

CHAPTER 5

AGAPE AND OTHER GREEK WORDS

We may give our human love the unconditional allegiance which we owe only to God. Then they become gods: then they become demons. Then they will destroy us, and also destroy themselves. For natural loves that are allowed to become gods do not remain loves. They are still called so, but can become in fact complicated forms of hatred.

C.S. Lewis, from *The Four Loves*

In a previous chapter, I mentioned that the word *love* in English can be used to describe a wide range of different states of being. For instance, it can be used to describe a mild sense of pleasure ("I *loved* that dessert"), or a general state of affection or affinity ("I *love* my country"), or a strong emotion for or attachment to something ("I *love* my car"), or even a deeper sense of one's connection with the Creator ("I *love* God with all my heart"). Given this wide range of meanings of the term—combined with the complexity of the feelings involved—it is no wonder why we find love so difficult to define.

This can be particularly problematic when we read passages in the Bible such as 1 John 4:7–8: "Let us love one another, for love is of God; and everyone who loves is born of God and knows God. He who does not love does not know God, for God is love." If we do not understand the difference between in-love feelings and true love, we will have a difficult time understanding the nature of God and how He can be love. We will also have difficulty following His commands to love our neighbors as ourselves (see Mark 12:31).

As members of the human race, we are the only creatures whom God made in His image (see Gen. 1:27). We are physical beings who live in a physical world, yet within each of us dwells a spiritual being—an eternal soul whom God made in His likeness. However, because we live in a fallen world—one that has been cursed due to the sin of every man and woman who enters it—we face a constant battle within ourselves between the physical and the spiritual. Our physical nature tells us to seek and strive for what makes us happy at the moment—the many pleasures of this life. But our spiritual nature, if we stop long enough to listen to its whispers, bids us to do what brings us lasting joy, and the decision is not always easy. One act feeds the body, while the other act feeds the soul.

This is the crux of the difference between in-love feelings and true love, which is of God. The state of limerence could well be one of the things to which the apostle John refers when He speaks of avoiding "the lust of the flesh" and "the lust of the eyes." Any actions we take to follow these desires are "not of the Father but … of the world" (1 John 2:16). Of course, this is not to say that *every emotion or passionate thought is wrong or constitutes limerence.* This is far from the case. If God is love and "in Him is no darkness" (1 John 1:5), then within Him lies all that is good, godly, and wonderful. Out of His love for us, He created every sense that we find pleasurable and enjoyable.

It is ironic that while we recognize that God gave us foods with delicious flavors and the taste buds to enjoy them, we feel uncomfortable about recognizing that He created us with senses that enjoy kissing, caressing, and making love. We skip over the fact that His first commandment to Adam and Eve was to "be fruitful and multiply; fill the earth and subdue it." As far as I know, there is only one way to accomplish that command. God created love and made us, as His crowning creation, to respond to that love; as we embrace it, we are able to love others. Loving God and loving our fellow humans are the greatest commandments and the purest pleasures this life can offer us. Partaking in these blessed actions is what brings us closest to heaven while on this earth.

At the same time, as C.S. Lewis observes in his book *The Four Loves*, the fact that "God is love" is not the same as "love is God." Lewis notes, "Every human love, at its height, has a tendency to claim for itself a divine authority. Its voice tends to sound as if it were the will of God Himself. It tells us not to count the cost, it demands of us a total commitment, it attempts to override all other claims and insinuates that any action which is sincerely done 'for love's sake' is thereby lawful and even meritorious."[34] Limerence is a false form of love, and regardless of how noble or divine we attempt to make it, it is not on the same plane as the other forms of love.

So what are these other forms of love? To find the answer, we need to turn to the pages of the Bible. However, before doing so we first need to examine four Greek words the ancients used to describe different states of what we today call love. As you review these words, remember that in many cases these different types of love will overlap and merge, and one might lead to another (or blend with another) at the same time.

Despite this difficulty, there are some general distinctions that can be made.

Eros (Intimate Love)

The writers of the Old Testament used several different Hebrew words for love, with the most common being *ahava* (meaning both love for God and love between people) and *chesed* (often translated as "loving-kindness). In the New Testament, there are three Greek words used for love: *storge*, *philia*, and *agape*. Interestingly, the Greek word for intimate or romantic love, *eros*—the one our society focuses so much attention on today—is never used.

Eros has been called passion, madness, and lovesickness. "Love at first sight" falls under this category, as does limerence, the state we discussed in the previous chapter. In Greek mythology, Eros was the son of the goddess Aphrodite, and it was believed that he was responsible for causing humans to form bonds of love—often illicitly. In preclassical Greece (750–490 BC), a cult sprang up that was dedicated to the worship of this god, and even today people continue to worship eros without reservation. As Lewis writes, "Eros, honored without reservation and obeyed unconditionally, becomes a demon. And this is just how he claims to be honored and obeyed. Divinely indifferent to our selfishness, he is also demoniacally rebellious to every claim of God or Man that would oppose him."

Lewis notes that of all the forms of love, eros by its very nature is the most godlike. Because of this, it is also the form of love that humans are most prone to worship. In a sense, people turn being in love into a sort of religion. The sad part is that eros, like its Greek namesake, is the most conniving and fickle of all forms of love. As Lewis writes, "We have all heard of people who are in love again every few years; each time sincerely convinced that 'this time it's the real thing,' that their wanderings are over, that they have found their true love and will themselves be true till death."[35] The truth is that relationships based on eros are in danger of failure:

> The couple whose marriage will certainly be endangered, and possibly ruined, are those who have idolized Eros. They thought he had the power and truthfulness of a god. They expected that mere feeling would do for them, and permanently, all that was necessary.... In reality, however, Eros, having made his gigantic promise and shown in glimpses what its performance would be like, has "done his stuff."

Lewis states that the only hope in eros is that it will transform into the greater forms of Christian love. This is accomplished when we are willing to "do the works of Eros when Eros is not present"—to take the rough along with the smooth and exhibit humility, charity, and grace when the romantic feelings are no longer percolating to the surface.[36] Moving beyond eros into the deeper forms of love will take hard work on our part and often supernatural strength from God.

Storge (Affection)

In classical Greek, *storge*, which can be defined as "affection or fondness," was used in reference to a mother's love for her children or the love of children for their parents. It is a vital form of love, especially for babies and young children, who have been known to die from the lack of it. In the New Testament, *storge* is used once in Romans 12:10, where it is translated "brotherly love," and twice with the prefix *a* (Rom. 1:31 and 2 Tim. 3:3), where it is translated "unloving."

In many cultures, as people grow older, they minimize affection and trade it almost exclusively for eros manifestations of love. However, as Lewis notes, affection portrays fondness, comfort, and ease, and it is a vital part of love: "Affection is the humblest love. It gives itself no airs. People can be proud of being 'in love,' or of friendship. Affection is modest.... It fits the comfortable, quiet nature of the feeling."[37] Affectionate love can be incorporated into the other forms of love and become the medium through which they operate from day to day.

Philia (Brotherly Love)

Philia, which can be defined as "brotherly love," is more commonly known today as friendship, though the use of the term in Greek was much broader than it is today. The philosopher Aristotle actually divided *philia* love into three types. The first was *friendships of utility*, which were formed without regard to the other person (such as the relationship between a buyer and seller). The second was *friendships of pleasure*, which were based on mutual enjoyment of those in the relationship (such as the friendships between close acquaintances). The third was *friendships of the good*, which were based on an appreciation of the character of those in the relationship (true friendships).

In the Bible, *philia* denotes this third type of friendship—a friendship that is founded in love rather than convenience, selfishness, or any other carnal reasons. A good example of this kind of friendship is the one Jesus shared with Lazarus. In John 11:3, when Lazarus fell ill, his sisters sent a message to Christ, saying, "Lord, behold, he whom You love [*philia*] is sick." By using the word *philia,* they were reminding Jesus of the close bond He shared with their brother and calling Him to come and heal him.

C.S. Lewis put a great value on brotherly love. He wrote, "Friendship, unlike Eros, is uninquisitive.... In a circle of true friends each man is simply what he is: stands for nothing but himself.... True friendship is the least jealous of loves. Two friends delight to be joined by a third, and three by a fourth.... In this, Friendship exhibits a glorious 'nearness by resemblance' to Heaven itself where the very multitude of the blessed increases the fruition which each has of God."[38] As Lewis concluded, true friendship is the instrument God uses to reveal the beauty of those in the relationship to each other.

Agape (Charity and Selfless Love)

In the New Testament, *agape* refers to a love that is charitable, selfless, altruistic, and unconditional. It is a form of love that describes God himself, for when John wrote that "God is love" (1 John 4:8), this was the word he used. It is the love God has for us and we have for God—a love that endures. As Lewis notes, "If love is to be a blessing, not a misery, it must be for the only Beloved who will never pass away."[39]

There is only one place where we can receive this type of true love, and only one for whom we should strive to love most fully. Even this action, however, depends on the love that God first gives to us. "We love [*agape*] Him because He first loved [*agape*] us" (1 John 4:19). This is the kind of love on which we can depend. It is the only love we should allow to fill us, so that we may then pour it out upon others.

Agape love is not easy, for it involves making ourselves vulnerable. It is a giving and humble love that seeks nothing for its own gain but rejoices in the giving. As human beings this is unnatural for us, for we tend to desire the gain rather than the loss, the receiving rather than the giving, and the joy rather than the pain. We tend to follow after the forms of love that promise instant pleasure. But in so doing we create an imbalance, for if our love for others is greater than our love for God, it "constitutes inordinancy."[40]

Agape—the love we receive from God—is what gives all other forms of love their meaning. So it is that while the four loves blend, merge, and combine, when the apostle Paul states, "The greatest of these is love" (1 Cor. 13:13), we can be sure that the type of love to which he is referring is the giving, sacrificial love of God, which we can only obtain with His power and through His Son, Jesus.

CHAPTER 6

THE BATTLE BETWEEN FAITH AND FEELINGS

Faith hath something firmer to stand upon than those ever-changing frames and feelings which … is fickle and frail, and changeth speedily from brightness into gloom.

Charles Spurgeon

Krissy had never been in an intimate relationship. After all, she had more important things to do. For the past few years, she had been working with a church mission, helping out at soup kitchens and women's shelters, and traveling during her school holidays to other nations, where she volunteered for a variety of projects. Krissy had a keen sense of purpose and knew she was called to serve God and others.

The summer she turned eighteen, after graduating from high school, she traveled to the Dominican Republic. There she volunteered with a group of other young people to better the conditions of schools in the country and, at the same time, to share the message of God's love with the students and teachers.

It was the most exciting time she had ever experienced in her life . . . for more reasons than one.

While Krissy was on this summer missions trip, she fell in love. A young man named Eric—tall, with dark hair and blue eyes—had taken notice of her the first day she arrived. She had never considered herself beautiful or outstanding in any physical way, so this young man's affections represented a new and welcome experience for her.

Eric had made it clear that she was his primary interest and the only reason he had decided to stay in the Dominican Republic beyond the first few days. Within a short time, his actions and attitude made it apparent to Krissy that he had virtually no interest in serving God and others. Yet in spite of this foundational difference, the two quickly developed a close and emotional relationship.

The more time the couple spent together, the more Krissy began to hope that things would work out between them. The very thought that the relationship might not last scared her. So she was pleased when Eric suggested that they go to California together when the mission trip was over. "I have a great job there and could easily support us both," Eric said. "As you know, I'm really only here because my parents said I had to see how other people live."

The idea of going to California with Eric was appealing, and as the end of the mission drew near, the thought of letting him go grew harder for her to bear. She loved the feeling of being in love. *I've already given a lot of time and help to others,* she reasoned. *It's about time I start making some decisions for me.*

Eric was the first to agree. "You can do good things in California too. There are lots of places where you could volunteer." Soon the idea grew into a concrete plan, and Krissy's previous life plans started morphing and changing. As they did, something else began to change. Krissy no longer felt joy in her tasks. The things that used to thrill her now seemed boring and mundane. Even one of the students commented to her in his broken English, "You seeming different."

What was wrong with her? On the one hand, everything finally seemed to be working out. She was in love and life was thrilling. On the other hand, she couldn't help feeling that something was missing—and that if she took Eric up on his offer she would never be able to find it again.

Finally, the week before the mission trip was to end, Krissy knew she had to make up her mind. She realized that whatever she decided would determine her entire future. Would she choose love or the life to which she knew she had been called? It was the most difficult choice she had ever had to make … but she made the right one.

Krissy said good-bye to Eric. There were tears. There were moments when she wondered if her choice was really the right one. It wasn't until years later, on her seventh mission trip overseas, when she met a man whose life goals and faith mirrored her own, that she finally knew for sure that she had made the right choice.

A Contract with God

Krissy's story, though unique in many respects, has one aspect that is common for most Christians: she had to confront a battle between her faith and her feelings. For the most part, this is something each of us will have to deal with our entire Christians lives. More often than not, our feelings will lead us on a different path than our faith would take us, and we will have to make a difficult decision based on something unseen.

Further complicating the problem is that our feelings will be enjoyable. Although they are intangible, by their very nature they will lead to something concrete and desirable. Faith, on the other hand, does not seem to provide us with many benefits—at least while we are on this earth. Living in faith requires us to adopt a mind-set that goes against the general stance of this world.

In the Bible, the author of Hebrews defines faith as "the substance of things hoped for, the evidence of things not seen" (Heb. 11:1). In the original Greek, the word translated as "substance" is *hupostasis*, which can also be translated "confidence," "assurance," and "title deed." In essence, *hupostasis* represents a contract between us and God—a title deed by which we are made bearers of the many promises He has given to us through His Word.

We cannot lose sight of the fact that our faith in the abiding promises of God is what gives us the ability to grasp those promises and please the one who gave them to us. God promises to give us good things—the very desires of our heart—yet He asks us to first delight ourselves in Him (see Ps. 37:4). The problem is that we often fear that if we let go of the things we can hold in our hands, we won't receive something comparable in return. In reality, it's like a child letting go of a plastic necklace in exchange for one of gold and pearls. However, it is still tough for us to release these things to God, because it requires having faith in the unseen.

The power of Christ's love is able to enter every area of our lives, including the areas of our emotions and feelings, to redeem them. Again, it's not that being in love is a bad thing. Many will testify that the times when they were in love were some of the most wonderful periods in their lives. However, if we depend only on feelings to help us make decisions—especially decisions as enduring as marriage—we will find that the fickle feelings fade and leave us with nothing but a failed relationship.

Feeling, Faith, and Fact

Even faith, though it is much more trustworthy than feelings, can disappoint us if we place our faith in the wrong things. Sometimes people who trust in God will say, "I have faith for this relationship." Yet just because we have faith in something we really want doesn't mean it's God's will for our lives. This is pseudo faith, and it will end up shaken. A little poem sums up the issue well:

> Three men were walking on a wall—
> Feeling, Faith and Fact.
> When Feeling had an awful fall,
> then Faith was taken back.
> So close was Faith to Feeling,
> that he stumbled and fell too.
> But Fact remained and pulled Faith back,
> and Faith brought Feeling too.[41]

When *feelings* fall and *faith* falters, it's the *fact* of Christ's love for us that endures. He has a plan for our lives, and He has the ability and desire to make our lives into something beautiful. All we have to do is place our trust in Him.

CHAPTER 7

A TRUE FOUNDATION

The rain descended, the floods came,
and the winds blew and beat on that house;
and it did not fall, for it was founded on the rock.

Jesus, from Matthew 7:25

As this point, I hope you see that the only sure foundation on which we can build a lasting relationship or marriage is not on limerence or eros, but on agape—the love of God and all that is His Spirit. Once we have this foundation in place, we can begin to establish a relationship that will stand firm when the storms of life come and attempt to sweep it away. We do this by using the right "building blocks," which the apostle Paul defines as "love, joy, peace, longsuffering, kindness, goodness, faithfulness, gentleness [and] self-control" (Gal. 5:22–23). We will examine each of these blocks—also known as the fruit of the Spirit—in turn and see how we can put them to work in our lives.

Love

As we have previously discussed, there are many different kinds of love, and there are also many different things that try to disguise themselves as real love but are in fact just cheap imitations. But how do we know which love we need to create a healthy and enduring relationship or marriage? One place Christians have often turned is 1 Corinthians 13, which is also known as the love chapter. In these thirteen verses, the apostle Paul clearly outlines what love *is* and what it *is not*.

In the King James Version of the Bible, the word used for "love" (*agape*) is *charity*. Unfortunately, when we think of charity today, we are more likely to picture an institution that does work among the needy than an actual expression of benevolent goodwill toward our fellow humans. To really pull out the meaning of this passage and determine what love means *today*, we need to transform these verses into modern terminology:

> If I could speak in other languages without making the effort to learn them and could speak in every language there is in all of heaven and earth, but didn't love others, I would only be making a lot of noise.
>
> If I knew everything that was going to happen in the future and was basically omniscient, but I didn't love others, what good would it do? Even if I had enough faith to speak to a mountain and cause it to move, none of that would matter one bit without love.
>
> If I gave everything I have to people in need, and if I were burned alive for telling others about God's love but didn't love others, it would have no lasting value.
>
> Love is patient. It doesn't mind waiting or being delayed. It keeps trying even when difficulties arise. It can put up with tough times—even being hurt or aggravated—and still not lose control or get upset.

Love is kind. It has a compassionate nature. It shows generosity and concern. It manifests sympathy when others suffer. It will go out of its way to help them in a spirit of courtesy and empathy.

Love is not jealous. It doesn't feel suspicious about a loved one or spouse, even when something happens that might arouse suspicion. It doesn't ask for disproportionate allegiance.

Love is not envious. It doesn't look at someone else's success and blessings and want to take it for itself. It doesn't compare qualities or possessions with others.

Love does not boast. It doesn't say or write things that bring attention to oneself in a proud manner. It doesn't constantly bring up personal achievements and successes.

Love is humble. It isn't proud. It doesn't carry an attitude of superiority and assume that it is better than others. It doesn't consider one's personal worth or abilities to be better than someone else's.

Love is not haughty. It doesn't act arrogantly or condescendingly.

Love is never selfish. It does not seek after its own wishes and desires while ignoring the needs of others.

Love is not rude. It is always kind of manner, not bad-tempered or impolite.

Love does not demand, "My way or the highway."

Love is not irritable. It doesn't blow up at others out of annoyance or exasperation. It will not do things to make someone else upset or angry.

Love forgives. It does not carry feelings of resentment around inside or harbor ill will.

Love is never glad when someone else is treated unfairly. It's happy truth wins out, and situations are solved in a loving manner.

As this list reveals, love is not based on strong emotions but in *consistent, concrete, and mindful choices*. If we truly want to love others as God wants us to love, we must make the decision to do the loving thing, regardless of whether it is easy or not.

In the Old Testament, God told His people that if they received harm, they were justified in taking an "eye for eye, tooth for tooth, hand for hand, foot for foot" (Exod. 21:24). But in the New Testament, Jesus told His followers, "A new commandment I give unto you, That ye love one another; as I have loved you, that ye also love one another" (John 13:34 KJV). This command is much more difficult to follow than the previous one, as Jesus explained in Matthew 5:38–42 (NKJV): "You have heard that it was said, 'An eye for an eye and a tooth for a tooth.'[a] But I tell you not to resist an evil person. But whoever slaps you on your right cheek, turn the other to him also. If anyone wants to sue you and take away your tunic, let him have *your* cloak also. And whoever compels you to go one mile, go with him two. Give to him who asks you, and from him who wants to borrow from you do not turn away."

Jesus told His followers that the greatest commandment God had given them was to "love the Lord thy God with all thy heart, and with all thy soul, and with all thy mind.... And the second is like unto it, Thou shalt love thy neighbour as thyself. On these two commandments hang all the law and the prophets" (Matt. 22:37–40 KJV). As Jesus made clear in the parable of the good Samaritan, our neighbor is anyone who needs our compassion and help (see Luke 10:25–37). If this is true, then how much more is our love deserved and needed by those on whom we bestow our fondest affections—those whom we claim to love?

It is simple to love when we have feelings to aid us, but it is the times when the emotions are not there and we still choose to make the decision to love that reveal whether our love is true.

Joy

A woman who was celebrating her fortieth wedding anniversary was once asked to relate the main thing that had carried her through the highs and lows of the past four decades. "There might have been a lot of things going on at any given time—raising six kids will do that," she replied. "But no matter what was going on, we knew how to laugh together. Sometimes, behind closed doors, we would be roaring in laughter together, and I think that's one of the main things that helped us over the years."

Joy is a vital component to a happy relationship. Even when things are not going perfectly, we can "rejoice always" and "in everything give thanks; for this is the will of God in Christ Jesus" (1 Thess. 5:16, 18). Nehemiah wrote, "The joy of the Lord is your strength" (Neh. 8:10), and we often need that strength to make it through a rough patch and end up better than ever before … and still together.

Peace

In Philippians 4:7, Paul promises that "the peace of God, which surpasses all understanding" will guard the hearts and minds of those who put their trust in Him. This trust must spill over into every area of our lives—including our relationships. God expects Christians to allow His Spirit lead us, and as we do so in a spirit of humble surrender, He will fill our hearts with perfect peace.

Long-suffering

Long-suffering is a manifestation of love that enables us to endure when things are difficult—*especially* when things are difficult—and continue on in a positive spirit. It is what allows a woman to pick up the dirty laundry left lying around the house day after day, knowing that her partner has a lot on his plate. It is what enables a man to overlook the fact that his wife always forgets to buy a certain food item that he would consider vital, because he knows she is usually multitasking when she goes shopping. Long-suffering is an understanding between couples that even though things won't always be perfect, that is OK because "love covers all sins" (Prov. 10:12).

Goodness

Parents will often tell their children to "be good" or to "not be naughty." But what does it mean to be good? We only know what is good in comparison to what is evil. Before Adam and Eve ate from the tree of the knowledge of good and evil, they could not understand the difference, because their state of innocence. But now evil surrounds us in this fallen world.

While many people try to be good on their own merits, as believers we understand that our human goodness is only an expression of God's goodness. We do not have any goodness in and of ourselves, but we must depend on the redeeming power of God's Spirit to make all things new within us. This is the only way we can manifest true goodness in our lives. In marriage, this will take more than mere human effort. Exhibiting goodness in our relationships will require the power of Christ to fill our hearts so we can make it a part of our very selves.

Faithfulness

As we discussed previously, faith plays an important part in building a positive and lasting relationship. When we trust in God's perfect plan for our lives, we are able to make choices that lead toward us fulfilling our God-ordained purposes. By exhibiting faith our faithfulness grows, and over time we develop a consistent nature of trustworthiness and devotion. These two characteristics alone are a recipe for a good marriage, but faithfulness also brings in dependability, loyalty, and stability. In 1 Corinthians 4:2, Paul writes, "It is required in stewards that one be found faithful." How much more so is faithfulness required in a healthy relationship?

Meekness

Meekness can be defined as "an attitude of humility toward God and gentleness toward men, springing from a recognition that God is in control."[42] Meekness is often seen as being synonymous with weakness; however, *Nelson's Illustrated Bible* states, "Although weakness and meekness may look similar, they are not the same. Weakness is due to negative circumstances, such as lack of strength or lack of courage. But meekness is due to a person's conscious choice. It is strength and courage under control, coupled with kindness."[43] Meekness requires effort to attain, and it is an important attribute for us to manifest if we desire to have a positive relationship.

Self-Control

When two people have been in a relationship for a long time, the tendency is often for them to "let it all hang out." Familiarity makes it easy for spouses to manifest the worst parts of their natures to one another, which can destroy a relationship. It is only when couples exhibit self-control that they are able to reign in their reactions and behaviors and keep them from negatively impacting their loved ones. Self-control is a fruit of the Spirit—which means it is a *positive* trait—and it makes it possible for God to imbibe His Spirit into our own.

As you reflect on each of the building blocks in the context of your most significant relationships, it might seem that some—if not all—are impossible for you to attain. However, the fact remains that He has called you as a child of God to reflect His Spirit and build your relationships around His principles of love and selflessness. This won't always be simple, but it is only by consistently exhibiting these traits that you can build a loving, positive, and lasting relationship. God's agape love is truly the *only* foundation solid enough for you to build an enduring and blossoming marriage upon it.

CHAPTER 8

TILL DEATH DO US PART

To have and to hold from this day forward, for better for worse, for richer for poorer, in sickness and in health, to love and to cherish, till death us do part, according to God's holy ordinance; and thereto I plight thee my troth.

Marriage vows from *The Book of Common Prayer*

Traditionally, marriage has been the "ultimate destination." For thousands of years of recorded history, finding a spouse and building a life together has been the mark of a fulfilled life—and bringing children into the world and raising them together completed the picture. But today, while many people still get married, more and more are considering other options. Some of these options include cohabitation, which we discussed in a previous chapter, and long-distance relationships, which are becoming more possible today due to the advent of the Internet and other forms of instant communication.

In some ways, relationships that vary from the traditional model might seem promising. After all, if love isn't just being "in love" and if building a healthy relationship requires manifesting the fruit of the Spirit into all aspects of our lives, why would we want to get married and sign up for all that hard work? Wouldn't it be simpler to just live together and hope to beat the breakup odds? Or maybe not live near each other at all, so we can maintain our own lives but still have a long-distance connection?

As we previously discussed, if present trends continue, more than half of all marriages in the United States will end in divorce. Given this, is marriage even worth it? What does a couple gain if they choose to commit to love each other "in sickness and in health, ... till death do us part"? What *are* the benefits to committing to each other in a marriage?

A Plethora of Pros

In fact, it is impossible to outline *all* of the benefits of marriage, because they truly are without number. As we discussed, the Bible tells us that God is love; because marriage is a manifestation of love, it provides the greatest opportunity for us to magnify the love of God in our lives. However, there are a few main benefits that we can identify in a healthy relationship. Note that while not all of these benefits will be manifested from the start of every marriage, these benefits will take root and cause the marriage to blossom as two partners strive to fulfill the greatest commandment by loving God and each other.

A Force for Good

Two people who combine their lives and sync their purposes together can become a force for good in this world. Instead of one person fighting for his or her dreams against the flow of the world, the two are now operating as a team—and there is strength in numbers. When two people merge their life goals and labors in this way, both will be able to realize their objectives more quickly and more easily.

Support

King Solomon wrote, "Two are better than one; because they have a good reward for their labour. For if they fall, the one will lift up his fellow: but woe to him that is alone when he falleth; for he hath not another to help him up" (Eccles. 4:9–10 KJV). There are many ways we can fall and many things that can cause us to trip—a bout of depression, losing a job, going through a difficult time with a child, facing an emotionally debilitating situation—but when these things occur, our spouses can provide wonderful support, picking us up and giving us a boost of love and strength until we are able to stand on our own two feet once more.

Security

Loving someone and being loved in return can give us a strong sense of security—especially if that person has committed his or her life to us. When that secure foundation is in place, it creates the opportunity for us to accomplish great things.

Humility

No one knows us as well as our spouses, because they see us up close and personal each and every day. While it is humbling to know that our spouses see us at our best as well as our worst—and love us anyway—it can serve to bring out the best in us.

Unselfishness

People who live alone cannot give away the last piece of pie or the best piece of chicken to someone else. That person doesn't have the opportunity to let another other person choose what to watch or where to eat out. It is only when we become part of a relationship and begin making decisions with another person that we begin to take into account our partners' preferences and desires. This helps us learn to become less selfish, and over time it serves to develop our character. Marriage provides this opportunity to grow in sensitivity to another person's needs and desires and to respond in a positive manner. Perception and responsiveness work both ways in a marriage. As we develop these traits to benefit our partner, we will receive the same in return.

Communication Skills

Interpersonal communication skills are important to develop and master and will serve us well regardless of what lifestyle or vocation we pursue. Whether we are housewives, stay-at-home dads and mothers, business executives, administrative assistants, project managers, pilots, or flight attendants, being able to communicate effectively with others is a vital strength. Having a spouse with whom we can communicate in a variety of situations (and under varying levels of pressure) can help us hone our communication skills.

It is a great blessing to have someone with whom we can communicate our needs and desires or whatever happens to be on our mind. We were all created with a need to communicate with other humans, and in a marriage we have the opportunity to pour out what is on our hearts, vent at the end of a rough day at work, or share good news about something that has concerned us. Communication is not only a skill but also a pleasure.

Safeguarding

Having someone to care for—and who cares for us—can help us build healthy habits. When we are on our own, there is no one to keep us accountable on a daily basis, and we can quickly slip into unhealthy habits. Marriage provides us with this accountability and gives our spouses the opportunity to help us in our weak areas, as we in turn help our spouses in their weak areas. When we realize that our habits and our health affect our spouses (and children), we are more likely to keep track of our actions and lifestyles.

Quality of Life

The only true joy in life is one that is shared with another, for a joy that is experienced alone dies a premature death. Being married enables us to share joy, gives us a better quality of life, and enables us to draw from vast resources of humility and love. It brings happiness, enjoyment, and a lot more fun into our lives. God created men and women to be together, and as we live our lives by that divine design, our quality of life improves, and we are able to fulfill a greater purpose than we could alone.

Eight Commandments for a Healthy Marriage

In the Old Testament, God gave the Israelites ten rules to follow to honor Him and receive blessings (see Exod. 20). In the same way, if we want to receive the blessings and benefits of a strong marriage, there are certain qualities we need to hone and put into practice. While there are no set commandments for marriage like the ones God gave to the Israelites, if there were they might look something like this.

1. Thou Shalt Put First Things First

It's a law in both the physical and spiritual realms that what we put first in our lives shows where our heart is and where our priorities lie. If we want to have a healthy marriage relationship, we have to put God first in all things. C.S. Lewis put it eloquently when he said, "The loves prove that they are unworthy to take the place of God by the fact that they cannot even remain themselves and do what they promise to do without God's help.… Even for their own sakes the loves must submit to be second things if they are to remain the things they want to be."[44] Only by keeping God in first place can we trust that love will remain strong enough to keep a marriage on course.

2. Thou Shalt Place Thy Spouse before Thyself

The only way our marriages are going to work is if we seek our partner's happiness before our own. This is not to say we become some sort of love slave—there has to be some give and take. However, by the look of many marriages these days, it seems that most people focus on the "taking" part of the deal, which can quickly lead a couple down the road to divorce.

3. Thou Shalt Be Willing to Tackle the Toughies

An issue that is hidden is an issue that isn't going anywhere any time soon. Whether it is a subtle difference of opinion or an out-and-out argument, problems first need to be addressed in order to be overcome. Many people today believe that if they ignore a problem, it will go away. They assume that things will just get better on their own, and they fail to take the step to communicate about issues. Having a willingness to communicate openly—and civilly—will create a healthy atmosphere of give-and-take and foster an environment in which solutions can be formed.

4. Thou Shalt Support Thy Other Half

When we take a vow of marriage, we are essentially making a decision to be incomplete without the other person. Our spouse has, in effect, become our other half in making life choices and goals. Just as we would not do anything to hurt ourselves, neither should we do anything to hurt or demean our "better half." Nothing weakens a relationship faster than criticism, gossip, or belittling our spouses, regardless of whether it is to them directly or about them to others. This is not to say we cannot disagree about issues or have differences of opinions, but we must seek to complement our spouses *through* our differences and still maintain our support *in spite of* them.

5. Thou Shalt Kiss

This might seem obvious to some and rather unimportant to others, but affection is a marital must—and not just kisses, but also cuddles, hugs, and tender touches. Such actions portray fondness, warmth, and loyalty. Even when everything is not going perfectly in a marriage, a kiss or warm embrace can be a sign that everything is going to be OK and that we're willing to seek solutions together.

6. Thou Shalt Show Respect

Respect is every bit as vital in husband-wife relationships as in parent-child relationships. Respect is a manifestation of more than just being in love, for it shows that we have taken the time to understand things that are important to our spouses and that we honor those things through our words and actions. In marriage, it is vital to respect our spouse's relationships with others (especially God), the times in which they need some space, and their feelings, perspectives, and choices. All of these signs of respect build a quality marriage.

7. Thou Shalt Show Consideration

Consideration is more vital in a marriage relationship than in any other relationship we will form. Sharing life with another person means not only our sharing our dreams and hopes, but also sharing our homes, our beds, our bathrooms, and even our closets. As we do this day after day, we can grow familiar with one another and begin to forget those things about the other person that make our lives so meaningful and wonderful.

To maintain an attitude of consideration, we have to regularly ask ourselves what our lives would be like if we lost our spouses tomorrow. Would they know just how much we love and appreciate them? If not, what could we do to show them that they mean more than the world to us? In addition, we must remember that even though we might know all of our spouse's specific preferences or opinions, everyone changes. We can't become so familiar that we begin to assume we know how our spouses will respond in every situation. Not seeking others' opinions will make them feel that we do not value their input.

8. Thou Shalt Laugh

There is no doubt that couples today bear a multitude of responsibilities. One or both will likely work, and as children begin to bless the household with love and laughter, they will also invite an endless extension of responsibilities. In many such stressful situations, laughter is truly a great medicine—and sometimes it is the only proper response. The ability to laugh when we feel like crying, shouting, exploding, or imploding will be one of the greatest assets to our marriage. Laughing at our own mistakes and about the issues together can keep us from fighting over them. Of course, there will be times when issues need to be addressed in a serious manner and laughter is not the proper response, but it is important to remember that the gift of laughter can be a blessing for any relationship.

Now and always, your marriage is what you and your spouse make it. So strive for a positive marriage—a quality one—that stands out in the world today. Make it a goal to build a marriage in which people can see that the love of Christ is obvious in your lives.

CHAPTER 9

GOALS OF THE GAME

The human loves can be glorious images of Divine Love.

C.S. Lewis, in *The Four Loves*

So now that we've discussed the benefits of marriage and the qualities that help build great marriages, is that *it*? Is a good and happy marriage the be-all and end-all? For some, it might be. However, as Christians we are called to more.

Marriage is not only a commitment to our spouse but also a commitment to God's plan for our lives together. As Christians, the relationship should extend far beyond the typical concept of marriage. A Christian marriage is meant to be an example of Christ's love for His bride and our love for Him in return. Such marriages are meant to be more sacrificial, more meaningful, more lasting, more wonderful, more satisfying, and more purposed than the average marriages we see today.

Two people in a marriage have amazing potential to further the redeeming work of Christ on earth. Although a marriage should include fun, enjoyment, pleasure, and companionship, it needs to represent two lives uniting together for a greater purpose. It is not only committing to support one another in our specific and unique callings, but also merging our passions together into something much greater than the sum of its part. This is what makes a marriage great—it is not only a blessing for those in the relationship, but serves as a testimony to others who see it as well.

In many ways, marriage is like building a house. We can choose to build a house with just the bare necessities—one that is barely big enough to fit those in the relationship, much less anyone else. Selfishness and focusing only on what we have to gain from the relationship will build such a "small-house" marriage. However, we can also choose to build big and have many rooms and amenities to spare. Using the building blocks of love, joy, peace, long-suffering, kindness, goodness, faithfulness, gentleness, and self-control will create such a "large-house" marriage.

Each of us has the power to "enlarge our borders." In biblical times, this phrase was used when a tribe extended its borders to bring in other tribes or peoples who wished to join forces with them or be protected by them. A strong marriage can act as a stabilizing force in the lives of not only the husband, the wife, and their children, but also in the lives of others. A marriage is a unique opportunity for couples to accomplish things they would not be able to do on their own.

So what does it take to create such a marriage? For Christians, a few main goals can help us carry God's redeeming power into our marriages and into our relationships with others as well. We will look at three of these "goals of the game."

Goal #1: The Partners Are Centered on Christ

There is a reason that Jesus told those who wanted to follow Him, "If any man come to me, and hate not his father, and mother, and wife, and children, and brethren, and sisters, yea, and his own life also, he cannot be my disciple" (Luke 14:26 KJV). In making this statement, was Jesus asking us to hate others? Hardly. He made it clear through His words and example that the most important thing to Him—and to us—was love. He even told us to love our enemies (see Matt. 5:44).

So what message is Jesus communicating here? At the time, Jesus had been traveling, and multitudes had begun to follow Him. He had been performing miracles of healing and had been teaching about the kingdom of God. Many in the crowd who had heard Him were eager for a new kingdom to arise—one that would break the chains of the Romans who ruled over them during that time in history.

But Jesus knew that was not an accurate picture of why He had been sent. Following Him wasn't going to be a walk in the park. It wasn't going to be perpetual blue skies and free loaves and fishes for all. Following God meant taking up a cross … and in that day and age—with a hill called Golgotha not far away—the people knew what that phrase meant. It meant death.

When we give our lives to God and accept Christ's blood as atonement for our sins, the next step is to take up the cross that God has called us to bear. Nothing else in life should compare with that calling—no friendship, no relationship, and not even the sacredness of marriage. *Nothing* should come before it. Of course, this doesn't mean that to be Christians we have to take vows of chastity and avoid all earthly relationships. What it does mean, however, is that we put God at the center of all of our relationships—and especially our marriage relationship.

This plays out in daily life in two ways. First, we make God a priority by taking time to read the Bible or other material that feeds our soul. We take time alone with God for our personal growth and time together for our growth as a couple. Second, we take time to pray together for our relationships, our families, our work, and anything and everything else! As we incorporate these steps into our lives and begin to center all of our beings on Christ, it leads us automatically into the next "goal of the game."

Goal #2: The Partners Are Progressing Spiritually and Personally

In a healthy marriage, both the husband and wife are experiencing personal growth. Both partners realize that their spouse is a special blessing—a priceless gift from God's hands—and should be treated as such. In the same way that having children makes us realize that God has entrusted a precious life into our care, our marriage relationships should make us realize that God has blessed us with our spouses, and therefore we should care for them as we know Christ would.

It is a great responsibility to be accountable for the concern, love, and compassion we give to our spouses. Hurtful words are like acids; they can easily destroy the fabric of any marriage. In Matthew 12:36, Jesus said that one day we will have to give account for "every careless word" that we speak. If this is the case, how much more will we have to give an account for the hurtful or unkind words we have spoken to our significant others? Rather than spew out hurtful words against our partner, we must choose to invest in their growth through support, prayer, encouragement, affection, and compassion.

It is critical that we treasure the one who walks beside us down life's road. We must make a commitment to invest not only in the *physical* well-being of our spouses (and children, if we have them) but also their *spiritual* and *emotional* well-being.

Goal #3: The Marriage Benefits Others

A third goal of marriage is that it should be a benefit to others. As we discussed at the beginning of this chapter, our marriages can serve as testimonies of the fruit of God's Spirit at work in the lives of His children. This doesn't mean we have to be perfect, or that our marriages have to be without problems. In fact, working through difficulties can refine a marriage and make it stronger than it was before. This serves as a greater testimony than an idyllic or problem-free marriage.

There is a certain mind-set in the world today that if something doesn't work right away, we should toss it out and get a new one. Sadly, this same perspective has crept into attitudes about marriage. Today, if problems crop up in a marriage and things don't always work right away, couples just get divorced and seek out a new marriage or relationship. As we discussed, this always ends in failure because no relationship is *ever* going to be perfect. Ultimately, people become more disillusioned and confused as to why their relationships "just don't work out." All the while, it is not the relationships themselves that are the problem but the mind-set that an immediate change is needed.

Just imagine the influence that one positive testimony of a strong and enduring marriage could have on such a person. That individual would see the couple's love and dedication and wonder what is different about them. It would cause that person to want to seek out what that couple has that he or she is missing. In the end, it could even point the person to developing a relationship with Christ.

The security and support of a strong marriage can act as a springboard and enable you to lead an inspired, focused, and purposed life and do great things for God. Your gifts can complement those of your spouse, and together you can create a force for good in the world. You can reach out together to people beyond your marriage—to those in your church, your ministry, your job, your neighborhood, your family, and even to others who cross your path over the years. You and your spouse can combine your efforts and visions and build a strong ministry together. The sky is the limit!

CHAPTER 10

HE SAID, SHE SAID

Contrary to what many women believe, it's fairly easy to develop a long-term, stable, intimate, and mutually fulfilling relationship with a guy. Of course this guy has to be a Labrador retriever.

Dave Barry, from *Dave Barry's Complete Guide to Guys*

As we have seen, marriage comes with many amazing benefits. But if this is true, why do so many marriages still end in divorce? Part of the problem is some fundamental differences in the way men and women approach issues and judge situations—differences that lead to disagreements and problems in a relationship. In this chapter, we will explore some of the diversity between the genders so we can understand how to grow in tolerance toward our loved ones. Acceptance is a stepping-stone to growth, maturity, and wisdom, and if we want our marriages to be blessings, we need to begin to recognize and accept these differences in our spouses.

Of course, before we can get to this acceptance stage, we first need to understand *why* these differences often get in the way of relationships between men and women. Dave Barry, in his classic manner, sheds some light on the subject by describing a dialogue between a couple named Roger and Elaine. One night, Roger and Elaine are driving home from a date when a thought occurs to her. Without really thinking about it, she says out loud, "Do you realize that, as of tonight, we've been seeing each other for exactly six months?" Elaine's proclamation is met with silence—a very loud silence in her mind—that causes both to begin thinking:

Elaine: *I wonder if it bothers him that I said that. Maybe he's been feeling confined by our relationship; maybe he thinks I'm trying to push him into some kind of obligation that he doesn't want, or isn't sure of.*

Roger: *Gosh. Six months.*

Elaine: *But, hey, I'm not so sure I want this kind of relationship, either. Sometimes I wish I had a little more space, so I'd have time to think about whether I really want us to keep going the way we are, moving steadily toward … I mean, where are we going? Are we just going to keep seeing each other at this level of intimacy? Are we heading toward marriage? Toward children? Toward a lifetime together? Am I ready for that level of commitment? Do I really even know this person?*

Roger: *So that means it was … let's see … February when we started going out, which was right after I had the car at the dealer's, which means … lemme check the odometer … Whoa! I am way overdue for an oil change here.*

Elaine: *He's upset. I can see it on his face. Maybe I'm reading this completely wrong. Maybe he wants more from our relationship, more intimacy, more commitment; maybe he has sensed—even before I sensed it—that I was feeling some reservations. Yes, I bet that's it. That's why he's so reluctant to say anything about his own feelings. He's afraid of being rejected.*

Roger: *And I'm gonna have them look at the transmission again. I don't care what those morons say, it's still not shifting right. And they better not try to blame it on the cold weather this time. What cold weather? It's 87 degrees out, and this thing is shifting like a garbage truck, and I paid those incompetent thieves $600.*

Elaine: *He's angry. And I don't blame him. I'd be angry, too.... I feel so guilty, putting him through this, but I can't help the way I feel. I'm just not sure.*

Roger: *They'll probably say it's only a 90-day warranty. That's exactly what they're gonna say, the scumballs.*

Elaine: *Maybe I'm just too idealistic, waiting for a knight to come riding up on his white horse, when I'm sitting right next to a perfectly good person, a person I enjoy being with, a person I truly do care about, a person who seems to truly care about me. A person who is in pain because of my schoolgirl romantic fantasy.*

Roger: *Warranty? They want a warranty? I'll give them a warranty. I'll take their warranty and stick it right up their ...*

At this point, Elaine breaks the silence:

"Roger," Elaine says aloud.

"What?" says Roger, startled.

"Please don't torture yourself like this," she says, her eyes beginning to brim with tears. "Maybe I should never have ... I feel so ..." (She breaks down, sobbing.)

"What?" says Roger.

"I'm such a fool," Elaine sobs. "I mean, I know there's no knight. I really know that. It's silly. There's no knight, and there's no horse."

"There's no horse?" says Roger.

"You think I'm a fool, don't you?" Elaine says.

"No!" says Roger, glad to finally know the correct answer.

"It's just that ... It's that I ... I need some time," Elaine says.

(There is a 15-second pause while Roger, thinking as fast as he can, tries to come up with a safe response. Finally he comes up with one that he thinks might work.)

"Yes," he says.

(Elaine, deeply moved, touches his hand.)

"Oh, Roger, do you really feel that way?" she says.

"What way?" says Roger.

"That way about time," says Elaine.

"Oh," says Roger. "Yes."

(Elaine turns to face him and gazes deeply into his eyes, causing him to become very nervous about what she might say next, especially if it involves a horse. At last she speaks.)

"Thank you, Roger," she says.

"Thank you," says Roger.[45]

When Elaine arrives home, as Dave Barry explains, she will lie awake all night and weep until dawn. Roger, on the other hand, will open a bag of Doritos, turn on the TV, and become deeply involved in a rerun of a tennis match between two Czechoslovakians he has never heard of. In the back of his mind he will have a feeling that something major was happening in the car, but since he has no clue what, he will decide it is better to just not think about it. The next day, Elaine will call her closest friends and for hours analyze every detail of what took place. This will continue, off and on, for weeks or even months. Meanwhile, Roger will one day be playing racquetball with a mutual friend of his and Elaine's, and he will pause just before serving and say, "Norm, did Elaine ever own a horse?"

Made in His Image

The book of Genesis tells us that in the beginning, God "created man in His own image; in the image of God He created him; male and female He created them" (Gen. 1:27). He made males and females unique and different, yet He made both in His image. When God saw that Adam was alone, He created Eve to be a helper to him (see Gen. 2:18). Some have said that God created Eve from Adam's rib because it was the closest bone to the man's heart. It is impossible to fully know why God chose to work the way He did, but it is clear that He made men and women to be together, to complement each other, to balance each other out, and to work toward a united purpose.

This is why the first step in truly loving our spouses is to accept and appreciate the differences between them and ourselves. Remember that those differences are likely what attracted us to our spouses in the first place—which gives credence to the popular saying that opposites attract. It is only later that those differences became points of contention in our relationships. Yet those differences are still what make life interesting and unpredictable.

The differences between men and women in general—and between husbands and wives specifically—provide both partners with an opportunity to progress in the area of tolerance. Again, acceptance is key in any relationship, because it is only when both members are working to bridge the differences with love, understanding, and tolerance that any progress can be made. If we are prepared to recognize these differences, acknowledge they are something we must (at the *very* least) learn to live with, and do the work required to face the challenges that these differences bring, we are already on the way toward strong marriages.

When a man and a woman bring together their differences and use them to balance each other out, a beautiful and colorful union can result, and life becomes more full and well-rounded than it would have been otherwise.

Common Differences between Men and Women

So what are some of the differences between men and women? While not a comprehensive list, the following includes many of the common differences that couples tend to notice between themselves and their spouses. As you review these items, keep in mind that these are general tendencies and will not necessarily fit every man or every woman. Just because most men and women tend to behave in a certain way does not mean *every* man or woman will be that way. Some women may have strong tendencies toward a certain characteristic that men tend to exhibit, and the same may be true for some men. In short, don't cut out this list and use it as a box in which to place people. Instead, let it be a helpful guide, and remember, "If anyone is in Christ, he is a new creation; old things have passed away" (2 Cor. 5:17). Strive to accept and expect even greater things from yourself and others, for with the redeeming power of Christ, nothing is impossible. With that said, here is the list:

- Men appreciate trust, respect, and acceptance; women enjoy hearing words of love and endearment.
- Men appreciate it when their wives manifest their love in physical ways; women appreciate it when their husbands manifest their love through words and affection.
- Men tend to be impartial in their interaction and affection with others; women tend to save their affection and attention for close friends and loved ones.
- Men don't enjoy partners who are too possessive or emotional; women crave the security of being possessed and wanted.

- Where a man's body goes, his mind follows; where a woman's mind goes, her body follows.
- Men are more sure of themselves and less likely to change their minds once a decision has been made; women are less sure of themselves and more open to change.
- Men tend to make decisions based on their physical needs or desires; women tend to make decisions based on their emotional needs or concerns about their families.
- Men think more about the physical repercussions of decisions; women think more about the emotional outcomes.
- Men look for physical outlets such as sports, hobbies, fresh air, and recreation; women look for emotional outlets such as friends who listen or supportive relationships.
- Men are more straightforward and direct; women are more complicated and less direct.
- Men enjoy giving and receiving practical gifts (things that can be put to good use); women enjoy giving and receiving romantic or sentimental gifts.
- Men are quick to take action; women are more cautious and weigh the options before making decisions.
- Men generally wait to address issues verbally, preferring to calm down and let time pass first; women want to communicate about issues right away, even if it's an emotionally volatile moment.

A healthy marriage is one in which both partners recognize their differences and use them to make the marriage more stimulating and exciting. It is one in which the members emphasize the things they have in common and do not allow their differences to keep them from uniting around common goals and pleasures. Remember that no difference is so insurmountable that it cannot be overcome through the love of Christ. His love can overcome any differences, His compassion can bridge any gap, His joy can fill any breaches, and His peace can encompass any chasm. His Spirit, and all that He brings to a marriage, can make any union—no matter how odd the couple—a beautiful one.

CHAPTER 11

LOST THAT LOVIN' FEELING?

You never close your eyes anymore when I kiss your lips.
And there's no tenderness like before in your fingertips.
You're trying hard not to show it, (baby).
But baby, baby I know it ...
You've lost that lovin' feeling, whoa, that lovin' feeling,
You've lost that lovin' feeling,
now it's gone ... gone ... gone ... wooooooh.

Mann, Spector, and Weil, from
"You've Lost That Lovin' Feeling"[46]

As we discussed in the previous chapter, we can turn the differences between ourselves and our spouses into strengths that will enable our marriages to be more stimulating and enjoyable. On the flip side, we can allow our differences to drive wedges between us and tear us apart. When that happens, we might find ourselves singing along with the Righteous Brothers, wondering where we lost that "lovin' feeling."

So what do we do if we find ourselves in this place? Are we simply destined to sing, "It must have been love, but it's over now"? When the emotions fade, is a marriage doomed to end? While we know marriage must be built on more than mere feelings, we will still have a difficult time dealing with the inevitable change of emotions that are bound to come at some point during the relationship. The story that follows illustrates just how tough these changing feelings can be to navigate.

The Ten-Month Mark

When Kylie was eighteen, she decided she would never marry. From experience, she had learned that the intense feelings that accompanied the beginning of a relationship always faded after ten months, at most. She did not want to deal with a lifelong commitment, knowing that the passionate emotions would not last. Nothing sounded worse to her.

However, a year later, Kylie began a relationship with a man named Chris. The relationship soon developed into a serious one, and after they had been together for about six months, Chris surprised her by proposing. Kylie remembered jokingly telling him that the relationship wouldn't last beyond the ten-month mark, but now it had potentially taken a serious turn. What would she do? Was she ready? She didn't know, and though she agreed to the engagement, she still worried about the future.

The couple ended up being engaged for two years. Although Chris was eager to go ahead with the wedding, Kylie wanted to be sure. She also wanted to find a solution for the inevitable change in emotions she knew would come. And, sure enough, it happened. She was distraught. *Am I incapable of truly loving?* she wondered. *Is every relationship doomed to die because I just can't keep these feelings?*

The problem was that everything else was great about their relationship. They shared common goals, and both of them had strong beliefs about loving and serving God and others. Chris was good with kids, and he loved her sincerely. Still, she couldn't help but think, *This isn't how it's supposed to be. I'm supposed to be forever in love with the person I'm meant to be with for the rest of my life.*

Ultimately, Kylie took the matter to God in prayer. She talked to God about her reservations, her fears, and her deepest dreams. At one point, she felt led to open her Bible, where she found the words, "Wherefore they are no more twain, but one flesh. What therefore God hath joined together, let not man put asunder" (Matt. 19:6 KJV). Kylie immediately recognized that God had blessed her with a caring and intimate relationship with a loving man who wished to be her life partner. He had placed them together, and here she was considering putting it asunder and breaking off the engagement due to a lack of feeling "in love."

Kylie also began to understand the ways in which her mind-set had been warped by the movies she had watched and the books she had read throughout her childhood and teenage years. Love wasn't solely about passion but about partnership. It wasn't only about great feelings but also about giving. It wasn't about finding "the one" but about learning to be "the one."

Kylie decided to commit to the relationship with Chris, walk down the aisle, and say "I do," and she never regretted her decision. While she knew she wouldn't always be ravished by her husband's very presence, she also knew that God had found her a soul mate—as He defined it, not her.

A Sacred Covenant

Unlike Kylie, many couples think their intense feelings for the other person will last forever. But at some point after the wedding bells have rung, they are faced with the reality that their feelings are not as intense as they once were. Yet the fact remains that when a man and woman decide to make the commitment of marriage, those two *are* "the one" for each other. Regardless of whether it was a shotgun wedding or a ten-year engagement, once a couple commits themselves to each other in the name of love, they become one flesh in God's view, and it is their responsibility to work toward becoming soul mates. Dr. Tim Gardner states,

> After the spark and the commitment of "till death do us part," we [have] to set our future course as husband and wife, and commit to remain soul mates. Certainly, we must talk and talk and talk—and pray and pray and pray. But we also [have] to learn healthy ways to resolve conflict, deal with and discuss marital expectations.... It doesn't sound a lot like "just falling in love for life," but that's how we learn to stay together—and thus experience what it really means to have a soul mate.[47]

Marriage is a covenant made under God, and He doesn't take covenants lightly. In today's world where promises are made lightly and broken without a second thought, it's not easy to wrap our minds around the concept of an everlasting agreement. However, when God made promises and established covenants, they were sound and lasting. Marriage should be viewed and lived out the same way.

Under the Old Testament laws, men had the right to "put away" or divorce their wives for various reasons (see Deut. 24:1–4). But when Jesus came to earth, He set a different standard for His followers. We see this in the Gospel of Matthew when a group of Pharisees—who were always hoping to trip up Jesus with their questions—came to Him and asked, "Is it lawful for a man to put away his wife for just any reason?" (Matt. 19:3).

The fact the Pharisees posed this question indicates that divorce was an issue even back then.

In response, Jesus, as usual, asked a question himself: "Haven't you read in your Bible that the Creator originally made man and woman for each other, male and female? And because of this, a man leaves father and mother and is firmly bonded to his wife, becoming one flesh—no longer two bodies but one. Because God created this organic union of the two sexes, no one should desecrate his art by cutting them apart" (Matt. 19:4–6 MSG).

The Pharisees shot back: "'If that's so, why did Moses give instructions for divorce papers and divorce procedures?' Jesus replied, 'Moses provided for divorce as a concession to your hard heartedness, but it is not part of God's original plan. I'm holding you to the original plan, and holding you liable for adultery if you divorce your faithful wife and then marry someone else. I make an exception in cases where the spouse has committed adultery'" (Matt. 19:7–9 MSG).

This answer seems to have bewildered Jesus' disciples. "'If those are the terms of marriage,' they said, 'we're stuck. Why get married?' Jesus answered, 'Not everyone is mature enough to live a married life. It requires a certain aptitude and grace. Marriage isn't for everyone. Some, from birth seemingly, never give marriage a thought. Others never get asked—or accepted. And some decide not to get married for kingdom reasons. But if you're capable of growing into the largeness of marriage, do it'" (Matt. 19:10–12 MSG).

In God's original plan, the covenant of marriage was meant to be a long-term covenant in which two partners could learn to grow and love. As Jesus said to the Pharisees, it was only because of people's hard-heartedness that God allowed divorce. He wanted them—and us—to live to a higher standard. The view of marriage, and the option for divorce, was meant to change with Christ's redeeming work on the cross.

Marriage Is a Gift from God

As Dr. Tim Gardner notes, "Marriage is a phenomenal gift from God; there should be a connection between wives and husbands that's deeper, more intimate, more personal, and more 'soul touching' than any other relationship we have. Married couples should experience a sense of being 'joined at the heart,' connected for a future purpose, and be 'more complete' with their mate than without them.... married couples should be soul mates."[48] But what about the person who claims, "I know that my marriage was not God's plan for me, so it's not my fault that we're no longer 'joined at the heart' and in love with one another. I have the right to do something about it."

Making a statement like this is as much as saying that God does not have the power to make everything right. Can a wrong choice that we've made change God's overall plan and purpose? Do we have the power to deride His sovereignty by our mishaps or mistakes? God is omnipotent, and in His wisdom and pure love He will work to perfect everything in the lives of His children—even a marriage that might have started off on bad ground or for the wrong reasons.

God has the power to redeem our marriages according to His perfect plan, which cannot be thwarted. It might take extra commitment, prayer, and even some (or a lot) of "elbow grease." But if we allow Him to take over, He can recreate our marriages. He can make them a thing of beauty and a testimony of His workings and mysterious ways.

CHAPTER 12

TIME FOR A TUNE-UP

Only if you have been in the deepest valley, can you ever know how magnificent it is to be on the highest mountain.

—Richard M. Nixon

At this point, you hopefully are convinced that it *is* possible to have a wonderful marriage. But does that mean you can just sit back, pray, and wait for God to work everything out as He molds you and your partner into perfectly loving soul mates? That would be nice, but it is about as realistic as that knight in shining armor waiting around every maiden's corner. As I've said, marriage takes work, and there may be an uphill climb ahead of you. But don't feel overwhelmed, because the summit has the potential of being breathtaking. In this chapter, I will show you seven steps you can take toward reaching those heights.

Step 1: Firm Up the Foundation

A marriage is only as strong as the foundation on which it stands. Just as in the ageless parable of the wise and foolish builders (see Matt. 7:24–27), where those who follow Christ's sayings are like those who build their houses on the rock, so the "house" of our marriage needs to be built on the solid-rock foundation of Christ's love.

Mutual attraction will fade. Children will grow up and move away. Circumstances will change. The waves of difficulties and the rains of testing will bear down on every foundation. It might take months or it might take years, but it is bound to happen. Any foundation other than Christ is shifting sand, no matter how strong it may appear to be at first. The result will be a broken-down house. That which was meant to shelter and bring joy will become a place of broken promises and sorrow.

If you've built your house on a foundation other than the solid Rock, you've likely already experienced this to some degree. Perhaps the marriage started off well, but the foundation shifted when other things began to take precedence. You may even feel that it is too late for you and your spouse—that the marriage can never be restored. But the beautiful thing about love—especially God's love—is that it's never too late to begin a life anew, or a marriage anew, and on the right foundation.

Make the decision to firm up your foundation and commit to each other once more—and do it before God. This doesn't mean you have to repeat your marriage vows or have a second wedding ceremony. Just say a simple heartfelt prayer, with the two of you agreeing before God and Christ in the midst of you. Or ask a pastor or church elder to pray over you. When you recommit to your spouse and consciously choose to make Christ the foundation of your relationship, you will have taken the first step in rebuilding your marriage. It will by no means be the last.

Step 2: Alter Your Perception

Have you begun to see your spouse in a particular way—and you know it's not a good perspective? Do those things that used to endear him or her to you now irritate you beyond belief? Have you stopped expecting good things from your partner because he or she has ceased to amaze you long ago?

If so, you need to alter your perception by making an effort to think and say positive things to your spouse. I know this is easier said than done, but there is great (and often untapped) power in positive thinking and expressing affirmation, appreciation, and encouragement. It is one of the greatest gifts you could give to your spouse, and all it takes is for one person to start the process. The following true narrative of a couple named Larry and Jo Ann illustrates this fact:

> Larry and Jo Ann were an ordinary couple. They lived in an ordinary house on an ordinary street. Like any other ordinary couple, they struggled to make ends meet and to do the right things for their children. They were ordinary in yet another way—they had their squabbles.
>
> Much of their conversation concerned what was wrong in their marriage and who was to blame—until one day when a most extraordinary event took place.
>
> "You know, Jo Ann, I've got a magic chest of drawers. Every time I open them, they're full of socks and underwear," Larry said. "I want to thank you for filling them all these years."
>
> Jo Ann stared at her husband over the top of her glasses. "What do you want, Larry?"
>
> "Nothing. I just want you to know I appreciate those magic drawers."
>
> This wasn't the first time Larry had done something odd, so Jo Ann pushed the incident out of her mind until a few days later.

"Jo Ann, thank you for recording so many correct check numbers in the ledger this month. You put down the right numbers 15 out of 16 times. That's a record."

Disbelieving what she had heard, Jo Ann looked up from her mending. "Larry, you're always complaining about my recording the wrong check numbers. Why stop now?"

"No reason. I just wanted you to know I appreciate the effort you're making."

Jo Ann shook her head and went back to her mending. "What's got into him?" she mumbled to herself.

Nevertheless, the next day when Jo Ann wrote a check at the grocery store, she glanced at her checkbook to confirm that she had put down the right check number. "Why do I suddenly care about those dumb check numbers?" she asked herself.

She tried to disregard the incident, but Larry's strange behavior intensified.

"Jo Ann, that was a great dinner," he said one evening. "I appreciate all your effort. Why, in the past 15 years I'll bet you've fixed over 14,000 meals for me and the kids."

Then, "Gee, Jo Ann, the house looks spiffy. You've really worked hard to get it looking so good." And even, "Thanks, Jo Ann, for just being you. I really enjoy your company."

Jo Ann was growing worried. "Where's the sarcasm, the criticism?" she wondered.

Her fears that something peculiar was happening to her husband were confirmed by 16-year-old Shelly, who complained, "Dad's gone bonkers, Mom. He just told me I looked nice. Even though I'm wearing all this makeup and these sloppy clothes, he still said it. That's not Dad, Mom. What's wrong with him?"

Whatever was wrong, Larry didn't get over it. Day in and day out he continued focusing on the positive.

Over the weeks, Jo Ann grew more accustomed to her mate's unusual behavior and occasionally even gave him a grudging "Thank you." She prided herself on taking it all in stride, until one day something so peculiar happened that she became completely overwhelmed her.

"I want you to take a break," Larry said. "I am going to do the dishes. So please take your hands off that frying pan and leave the kitchen." (Long, long pause.) "Thank you, Larry. Thank you very much!"

Jo Ann's step was now a little lighter, her self-confidence higher, and once in a while she hummed. She didn't seem to have as many blue moods anymore. "I rather like Larry's new behavior," she thought.

That would be the end of the story except one day another most extraordinary event took place. This time it was Jo Ann who spoke.

"Larry," she said, "I want to thank you for going to work and providing for us all these years. I don't think I've ever told you how much I appreciate it."

No matter how hard Jo Ann has pushed for an answer, Larry has never revealed the reason for his dramatic change of behavior, and so it will likely remain one of life's mysteries. But it's one I'm thankful to live with.

You see, I am Jo Ann.[49]

Altering your perception has the power to change not only your spouse's life for the better but also your own. With God's help, you can alter the situation in your marriage, and when you choose to do so, you will have taken the next step in tuning up your relationship.

Step 3: Create the Magic

Do you feel you've lost the magic long ago? If so, perhaps you've just stopped looking for it. When was the last time you brought home flowers … just because? Or placed candles on the table at dinnertime? Or asked a family member or friend to look after the kids for the evening? Or snuck a kiss when passing through the room? Or just looked deeply into your loved one's eyes without saying a word? Here are some other ways to create the magic at home, and they don't cost much more than time and thought:

- Choose a simple outdoor activity that you both enjoy doing together, such bicycling, roller-blading, or even walking.
- Take a drive together (like people used to do) through a park, or a lovely neighborhood, or outside of town if you're close enough.
- Put on some music and cuddle as you listen to it together.
- Check out inexpensive concerts, museums, or galleries in your area.
- Go to a cafe or bookstore and read softly to each other, or just enjoy some light conversation.
- Make dinner together. Don't forget to create ambience!
- Play a board game together. (It's OK if you get a little competitive, as long as you kiss and make up afterward.)
- Share stories of your childhood with each other.
- Start a blog and post stories of how you met, what you enjoy doing together, some great moments as a couple, and lots of pictures!
- Exchange massages.
- Watch a fun romantic movie, complete with popcorn and cuddles.
- Take a bath together. Take your pick of bath salts, rose petals, or candlelight to complete the effect.
- Go on a picnic and watch the sunset (or sunrise, if you enjoy early mornings outdoors).
- Wash your car together. Ensuing water fights are allowed.
- Go outside after dark to stargaze.

- Spend some time looking through photo albums of your early years together.
- Read about plants or trees and choose one that represents your relationship. Go buy it, plant it, and take care of it together!
- Choose a home improvement project and work on it from start to finish together.
- Pretend you are tourists in your own city and "see the sights." Take pictures of everything you see.
- Let the other person decide what you will wear for a romantic evening at home.
- Make breakfast and feed it to each other in bed.
- Create a romantic ritual—something you repeat every week or month.

All it takes is a little effort to put the magic back into your relationship. When you tune up your marriage in this way, you will be ready for the next step.

Step 4: Get to Know Each Other

Remember the early days of your relationship when you would talk into the wee hours of the morning, or wake up early to discover something new together, or look forward to seeing the other person when you were apart? Remember the fun side of your spouse before the marriage began to sag in the middle and fray at the edges? Do you want to get to know that person again?

If so, you need to take the time to get reacquainted with your spouse. Do you still know his or her deepest hopes and dreams? Do you know what makes him or her upset or disappointed? Do you know what he or she feels would make your marriage more fulfilling and complete? So often when a marriage ends, one or both partners will say, "He never really knew me" or "She never cared about what I felt inside." You don't have to let this to happen to your marriage.

Care.

Ask.

Then show your love by reaching into each other's hearts and holding on tight!

Step 5: Talk about It!

Are there issues that have been labeled "hands off" that you don't discuss, even though they stare you in the face every day? Have these unresolved issues caused everything to look huge and insurmountable in your relationship? If so, schedule some time to talk about these things. You don't need to tackle them all in one discussion session, but get the ball rolling to sort through the issues and keep them from festering inside. As you talk, perhaps you will discover your partner's reasoning for why he or she does certain things. Or maybe you will realize that something you thought was major wasn't such a big deal after all. As you follow this step and begin scaling these issues, the future ones that are bound to come along won't seem so overwhelming after all.

Step 6: Think Professionally

If you hold a job of any sort, you know that training was required before you could fulfill the duties of that position. Perhaps it took months or even years of education and training before you could do it well. If you are ambitious and seek to remain on the cutting edge, you most likely have to continue your training in some way by taking relevant classes, studying online, or buying and reading books. Regardless of the field professionals are in, they must continue learning.

Marriage is no different. If you want to fulfill your role as a husband or wife—and you want your spouse to do the same—you both need to apply time and energy into making it cutting-edge and extraordinary. You need to adopt the same attitude about your marriage as you would about your professional life or your personal goals. It's not going to happen by itself. So be creative and energetic, and don't quit!

Step 7: Don't Forget to Say "I Love You"

Words have power, and those three words—"I love you"—are some of the most powerful that can be spoken. But there are other ways to express your affection as well. Here are just a few ideas to get you started:

- You light up my life.
- You make me a better person.
- Your love means the world to me.
- You help me feel I can be more.
- Thinking of you makes me smile.
- I still love your smile.
- I love loving you.
- When we're close, my heart is full of your love.
- I love your voice.
- Thank you for taking care of me.
- You're my angel.

Get creative, not just in your actions but also in your words. Put Christ at the center of your relationship, follow these tune-up steps, and watch what happens in your marriage. And remember that while you won't climb the mountain in a day, or a week, or even a month or a year, the goal isn't necessarily arriving at the summit but enjoying the climb *together*.

CHAPTER 13

BEYOND REPAIR?

To forgive is to set a prisoner free and discover that the prisoner was you.
Lewis B. Smedes

Elaina tapped the toe of her designer shoe as she stood over the carpet samples strewn across the room. It seemed as if there was a sample for every design imaginable. She was a petite woman, and while some would say she was beautiful, no one would call her sweet. Driven, yes. Successful, definitely. Lovable and charming … no.

With her lips pursed, she began talking to herself. "Let's see, I met with the Jennerlings, and I provided the proposal to the Manhattans."

She turned to her assistant. "I just need to do one more thing. Bring me yesterday's reports."

Dorothy was accustomed to her boss talking *at* her rather than *to* her. She responded quickly with an audible "Will do," and went to retrieve the reports.

When she returned, Elaina began flipping through the pages and started talking somewhat curtly to Dorothy about efficiency. It's not that Elaina was a cruel woman, it's just that she had zero tolerance for mistakes. Dorothy had been with the architectural firm for almost three years, but she was still only marginally efficient at her job. She had lasted longer than any of Elaina's previous assistants because she knew how to discern her boss's moods and accommodate her. Elaina would never admit it, but she depended on Dorothy to take care of everything for her.

Elaina was not the best at expressing her feelings. She realized many years ago that if she wanted to get ahead, she had to part with her sensitive side. She was a woman in what was typically considered a man's line of work, and she had to fight, bite, and crawl to get ahead. Unfortunately, this same attitude transferred to her love life. She went through men like athletes go through shoes. Most guys just couldn't handle her outspoken and dominant side. Friends had set her up with guys on many occasions, but she could never make it past the first few dates.

At first, men would consider her strong demeanor to be sexy. But before long they would grow tired of her controlling ways and her miserly nature. She made a great deal of money, but she was picky about the people with whom she would spend it. Most guys would disappear when they learned she had planned everything in her life down to the smallest detail.

On this day, Elaina had once again been set up on another blind date. She was secretly hoping this evening would be different, though she was careful not to raise her expectations too high. She made sure she didn't leave work earlier than usual, as she was proud of always putting in the hours. Of course, this put her at a disadvantage in "girl time," for, as everyone knows, it takes a good hour and a half to get ready for a date. This didn't bother Elaina too much, though, because she operated on "guy time." She was always punctual and got dressed very efficiently.

Within ten minutes of arriving home, Elaina was brushing her teeth and checking her clock in the bathroom. She had exactly fifteen minutes to spare. She expertly put on her makeup, making sure to apply it evenly and with exact lines on her eyes. She put on her black cocktail dress and went out with her hair cascading down to her waist. She was a spicy Russian with cool blue-green eyes that contrasted with her raven-black hair. She was what people call exotic.

As she was finishing up, the doorbell rang. Alexander, her date for the evening, had arrived.

Alexander had been growing more nervous as he made his way up the elevator to the penthouse. He had heard rumors that Elaina was an ice queen, but he was hoping those rumors were untrue. He wasn't afraid of a little feistiness in a woman, nor was he intimidated by a woman who earned a good living, but he couldn't handle a woman who was demeaning.

After what sounded like a series of locks being opened, Elaina popped her head out the door, took one look at the five-foot-three Alexander, and promptly slammed the door in his face. He heard footsteps and the sound of a television turning on. Incredulous, he waited at the door, thinking that her first reaction must have been some kind of mistake. He waited a little longer, and then he heard the sound of a microwave and what sounded like popcorn popping.

She really just left me out here, Alexander said to himself. Finally, he stormed off.

Elaina waited a few moments before peeping her head out the door. She exhaled a sigh of relief and then called down to the doorman. "Please do not allow that man to come back up to my apartment," she said. The doorman politely inquired if there was a problem, to which she responded, "Nope. Not now."

Alexander couldn't understand why he couldn't get Elaina out of his head. He waited a couple of days, and then he called her back and asked for another date. Elaina was shocked that he would want to see her again after their last encounter, and she was intrigued that he had the guts to call her back. She finally agreed to having dinner out.

The dinner was fabulous. The two chuckled and enjoyed each other's company. As the dates continued and they got to know each other better, they became mesmerized with one another. Soon they were married.

After a few months of marriage had passed, Alexander found that he was attracted to a coworker. He was able to resist the temptation for a while, but it was a struggle because he was lacking intimacy in his relationship with Elaina. He worked late, and on most nights Elaina didn't wait up for him.

Late one night, Alexander finally succumbed and cheated on Elaina. He felt so bad afterward that he knew he had to confess what he had done. So twenty-four hours after the incident, as the two sat down to watch their weekly shows, he blurted out that he had cheated and had a one-night stand. He apologized and said it would never happen again.

Elaina felt betrayed. She had opened up to this man and given him everything, and this was how he repaid her! She was hurt and furious with him. Weeks went by before she even spoke to Alexander. When she finally did, she told him that if he wanted to save the marriage, he needed to meet her at the office of a Christian marriage therapist the following day.

Elaina and Alexander began therapy, and after a few months, they found that they were able to move past the hurt and betrayal and trust each other in a new way. They were able to work through not only the infidelity but also many of their other marital issues. Their marriage became stronger than it ever had been before.

The Root of Failed Marriages

Infidelity is an issue that more and more married couples are facing today. In a recent article on why couples cheat, Lindsay Shugerman outlines some surprising statistics:

> According to the *Journal of Couple and Relationship Therapy*, approximately 50 percent of married women and 60 percent of married men will have an extramarital affair at some time in their marriage. And since it is unlikely that the people having affairs are married to each other in every case, the current statistics on the percentage of married couples who cheat on each other means that someone is having an affair in nearly 80 percent of marriages. These numbers represent a huge jump in the past decade. A University of California study in 1998 reported that 24 percent of men and 14 percent of women had had sex outside their marriages. In only 10 years, those numbers have more than doubled.[50]

Discovering a spouse's illicit affair is an obvious reason to divorce—some sources say it's the most common reason—but it is not the only one. Some other reasons couples give for why they choose to divorce include communication breakdowns, financial issues or difficulties, child-rearing issues, and health issues.

Looking more closely at these reasons, it is apparent that selfishness and a lack of true love are at the root of most failed marriages. When married people choose to *have an affair*, they make their decisions based on themselves and what they want. They are definitely not focusing on the needs of their spouses, who are left in the dark and eventually wind up being hurt and distraught. *Communication breakdowns* usually come about when couples choose not to take the humbling steps of communicating to each other in an attitude of acceptance and love. *Financial difficulties* are a common occurrence in today's economy, yet it is only when couples allow those issues to drive wedges between them that finances begin to look insurmountable. *Child-rearing issues* are often caused by one or both partners refusing to accept the mind-set, perspectives, or suggestions of the other. Allowing *health problems* to be a reason for divorce is another distressing manifestation of selfishness. "In sickness and in health," as we all know, is one of the sacred marriage vows.

It is common and typical for people to adopt these attitudes. After all, it goes against the human grain to choose elements such as love, forgiveness, understanding, grace, faith, and trust. In fact, these attributes are nigh impossible for anyone to attain without the grace and power of Christ. However, in taking on His Spirit, "all things are possible to him who believes" (Mark 9:23). For this reason, it is critical to remember: Actions can be forgiven, hurts can be healed, rifts can be mended, difficulties can be overcome, differences can be resolved, and love can be renewed.

These heart-healing solutions do not come naturally, and they are often not seen as logical. However, they are not unnatural or illogical; rather, they are *super*natural and *supra*logical. In other words, in many cases they only make sense through the eyes of faith and are only possible through the love and redeeming power of Christ.

A Word on Forgiveness

Forgiveness is a powerful tool that can be used to restore a broken and suffering relationship.[51] It can act as a healing elixir for a hurting heart or as a fountain that washes clean the sullied actions of another. While it is employed differently in every situation, the more trying the circumstances, the more powerful the results will be when a person chooses to make the difficult decision to forgive.

Jesus himself taught us to pray, "Forgive us our debts, as we forgive our debtors" (Matt. 6:12). This indicates that our forgiving others is directly related to God's forgiving us. In this way, forgiveness is synonymous with love. It is key to building a solid and secure marriage, but it requires a level of maturity that is often sadly lacking in many relationships. Making the choice to forgive is especially difficult in situations where a spouse is dealing with issues of infidelity and other breaches of trust.

Perhaps it is this difficulty that makes forgiveness so powerful when it is put into practice. It truly has the power to change hearts and minds and restore what once seemed irrevocably broken. Given its power, why then are so many couples hesitant to take the necessary steps to forgive and extend grace and mercy to their partners? In *A Long Way East of Eden*, author Pete Lowman offers these insights:

> In any relationship, we are occasionally going to lose control. Anger, carelessness and jealousy are realities; and families break up because of inability to deal with these things. Inability to forgive generates inability to apologize or, indeed, to resolve anything.... Either the marriage will break, or we must learn to accept, and forgive, our partner as (s)he is. The skills of compromise, apology and forgiveness are essential to a long-term relationship. But they don't come easily, and they do demand practice.
>
> There are other ways of thinking about forgiveness. "I don't get mad, I get even," seems widely acceptable. "In a secular age," writes Blake Morrison, "Christian notions of atonement, redemption and 'turning the other cheek' seem archaic, even craven.... To forgive is to be 'soft.' It's to let yourself be walked over. You only do it if you're lacking in self-assertion and self-respect." [There is] a clear correlation between commitment to the value of forgiveness and commitment to Christian faith. This is not surprising; Christ's cross embodies the overwhelming importance of

> our forgiveness by God.... Faith in the cross leads to an understanding of love conducive to lasting relationships....
>
> For Nietzsche, the dynamic of self-sacrifice, apology and forgiveness was precisely one of the things that made Christianity redundant, since the individual's will to power was the only reality. Christian ethics, he declared, was the morality of the weak, revealing no more than an "inability to take revenge."[52]

Clearly, any of us who have undertaken the challenge to forgive know that it is anything but an "inability to take revenge." In fact, as I stated previously, without Christ's love at work in our hearts, it would not even be possible. Forgiveness means allowing ourselves to break and then giving those broken pieces to the Master Potter so He can rebuild us again. This is what makes forgiveness so freeing—when we are willing to go through the process of breaking, we are released from the anger and bitterness that held us in captive in the past. As has been aptly said, holding on to resentment means allowing the one you won't forgive to live rent free in your head.

Forgiveness is more for us than it is for the other person who wronged us. So if resentment has you bound and bitterness has taken root in your heart, choose to forgive. Make the decision to give the entire situation—no matter how hurtful or how deeply it has affected you—over to God. Allow Him to make you whole and work the situation out for your good, as He has promised to do (see Rom. 8:28).

A Threefold Cord

Regardless of the exact circumstances in which you find yourself or the particular difficulty you face in your marriage, there is always hope in the power of God's agape love. His love, which goes beyond human understanding, will rest within your heart and heal, restore, and make you new. This will take time—perhaps more time than you expect—and it might take continued counseling. It will definitely require prayer, commitment, and a conscious decision to try.

Never doubt that God's love is greater than your lack of it. Only He can truly heal your hurts and redeem to himself what you thought was lost forever. As the author of Ecclesiastes states, "A threefold cord is not quickly broken" (Eccles. 4:12). When you, your life partner, and God come together, you will create a strong and lasting relationship that will not easily be broken.

CHAPTER 14

AND THEY LIVED HAPPILY EVER AFTER

I just want to live happily ever after, every now and then.

Jimmy Buffett

Unfortunately, as the woman in Dave Barry's narration mentioned, there is no knight in shining armor waiting to ride up and take us away on his white horse. There is no fair maiden like Snow White waiting for our kiss to bring her back to life. In spite of what filmmakers have attempted to tell us, when people fall in love, their days are not always carefree and filled with perpetual bliss. These movies always end with the couple gazing lovingly into each other's eyes and holding hands as they ride off into the sunset. What they fail to mention are the subsequent years of raising children, navigating finances, facing crises, and making decisions such as who is going to join the PTA and whose relatives they are going to stay with during the holidays.

For the most part, the movies we watch, the books we read, and the songs we listen to do not accurately portray the way our lives are going to work out. The wedding ceremony, where we stand before the aisle and exchange vows in front of a hundred or more people, is only the beginning. Marriage is a whole lot more. It truly is "for better for worse, for richer for poorer, in sickness and in health, to love and to cherish, till death us do part." While it's easy to say "I do" to these scripted lines, without God's help we cannot fulfill any pledges to live out this type of love for our spouses day after day for "as long as we both shall live."

However, with God's help, we *can* have a happily ever after. Of course, this will look much different than what today's filmmakers portray on the big screen. It will not involve living in a great castle surrounded by magic and splendor. Marriage is much different than a castle existence. In fact, in the world of today, a Christian marriage might be better viewed as a scene on a battlefield, where a husband and wife face life in the trenches together.

Today, there is a war being waged against true love and its many facets. Peace is being slowly eroded away as our lives move faster and faster. Joy is being zapped, as evidenced by the numerous cases of depression in our modern world. Longsuffering has lost out in favor of impatience. Gentleness has been exchanged for force and violence. To stand for the true meaning of love is to stand against the flow of this world, and those who do not want to accept that there is such a thing as godly and righteous love will resent us for it.

Yet there are some who want to see this kind of love manifested. This is why you and your spouse's marriage has the potential to be "a city that is set on a hill" that "cannot be hidden" (Matt. 5:14). If you let the light of your love "so shine before men," people will "see your good works" (Matt. 5:16). As they witness the work of a good marriage—a couple who is living and raising their children in the nurture and admonition of the Lord—they will sit up, take notice, and "glorify your Father in heaven" (v. 16).

The Power of a Positive Model

While you might never be a marriage counselor, your example of a godly marriage can be just what another couple needs to see and aspire to adopt themselves. This was certainly true in the case of a couple named Grace and Carl.

Grace had pretty much decided she would have to call their marriage quits. For years she had tried to build a positive and strong marriage, but she had come to the realization that there were just too many divisive problems. It had taken her three years to convince Carl to start attending church, but she knew that this was not the real issue. It was a matter of the heart.

Carl would dutifully sit next to her in church every Sunday, but then he would go back to his perpetual lifestyle of video games, watching TV, and basically neglecting her and his family. No matter how many times she requested, he would never take any of their three children out to the park to play ball, or offer to take over so she could have a break, or even give a positive word to her or their children.

Although they both worked, Grace felt she worked a double shift. When she came home in the evening, her time was filled with preparing meals, cleaning the house, paying the bills, and performing the many tasks of running a household and a family. All of this was tiring, but the most difficult part for Grace was that their children did not have a godly father figure to look up to who manifested the traits of forgiveness, kindness, patience, meekness, and most of all, fatherly love.

Grace and Carl had gone through a period of separation about five years into their marriage, when she had become distraught over his emotionally negative attitude toward their children. It was a time of soul-searching and spiritual growth for Grace, and she assumed it would be the same for her husband. When they got back together later that year, she had high hopes for the next stage of their relationship. Unfortunately, Carl had not changed one bit. If anything, he was more sullen and pessimistic.

Four years had passed since that separation, and with three children to care for and no change on the horizon, Grace was seriously thinking about a permanent separation. She hated the thought. She didn't know how she and the kids would be able to survive, but at the same time she knew her life couldn't go on like this. She was beginning to fear for herself and her children. It wasn't that she worried Carl would physically abuse them, but his attitude was bringing down the whole spirit of the house. There was no joy, no enthusiasm, and no love.

One day, Grace was at a summer barbeque with her friend Mary, who had just returned to her church after spending some years away in another state. She watched with sadness as Mary's husband played tag, hide-and-seek, and other games with the younger kids on the lawn. He spoke kindly to his wife, offered to get her some lemonade … and just did the things Grace expected a husband and father would do.

"Eric is really good with your kids, isn't he?" Grace said. "I wish I had that."

"Had what?" Mary asked.

"All Carl does is sit around and watch TV or play video games," Grace replied. "He hardly ever talks to the kids." Mary hadn't even noticed that Grace's husband was not at the barbeque.

During the next few weekends, Grace and the kids spent a lot of time with Mary and Eric's family, and Grace confided more of her story to her friend. At one point, Mary suggested that perhaps Eric could talk to Carl. Grace just shook her head sadly. "I doubt that is going to work," she said. "Both the pastor and his assistant have spoken to him at my request, but nothing has changed. I think he has to *want* to change, and it doesn't look like he does. I don't think there's any hope in talking to him."

"Well, then we'll pray for the situation," Mary offered.

"Thanks," Grace replied. "I've been praying for years and nothing has changed, but I do appreciate it."

That evening, Mary's seven-year-old son, Caleb, approached her after dinner. Carl, as usual, was playing a video game in the same room, aiming to reach the next level. "I really like Mr. Eric," Caleb said.

"Oh yeah?" said Grace. "Why is that?"

"Well," said Caleb, "when his kids do something bad and he has to correct them, he doesn't get angry or mean. He's not mad at them, and he plays with them again afterward."

Tears came to Grace's eyes. "Yes, honey, that's how it's supposed to be," she answered softly. She didn't realize that Carl had heard the exchange and that something had begun to speak to his heart.

The following weekend, when Grace asked, as she usually did, if he wanted to come along to Eric and Mary's house, she was surprised to hear him say yes. He didn't do much while he was there besides observe the activities and goings on. He mainly watched Eric interact with his children.

You might guess the rest of the story, but I'll tell it anyway. The change in Carl didn't happen in a day, and there were times of regression, impatience, and mistakes. But step-by-step Carl began to learn what it meant to be a loving husband and father. Grace decided against the separation she had been considering.

It was a happily ever after. It wasn't perfect, nor was it something you would likely make a movie about. But the two were happy and had true love—God's love. In the end, that was all that really mattered.

A Love for Eternity

Perhaps you are just at the beginning of your marriage road, tentatively taking your first steps of commitment. Or perhaps you've been married for decades and have weathered many storms of life together. Maybe you consider your marriage to be a happy one, or maybe you feel you are at the end and have no hope.

Regardless of where you are in your relationship, remember that true love—God's agape love—has the power to take something good and make it wonderful, and it has the power to take something bad and make it beautiful. But perhaps the best thing about God's love is that it is ever after and beyond … for eternity.

Who wouldn't say yes to a love like that?

EPILOGUE

There is going to be a wedding reception one day that will leave even the most original and outstanding earthly ceremony in the dust. The Bridegroom will come out of His chamber rejoicing, for He has completed the race and won His bride. The bride will be eager and waiting, for she has kept her lamps burning and has not given up waiting for the Bridegroom to arrive. This will be the marriage of the Lamb, described by the apostle John this way:

> And I heard as it were the voice of a great multitude, and as the voice of many waters, and as the voice of mighty thunderings, saying, Alleluia: for the LORD God omnipotent reigneth. Let us be glad and rejoice, and give honour to him: for the marriage of the Lamb is come, and his wife hath made herself ready. And to her was granted that she should be arrayed in fine linen, clean and white: for the fine linen is the righteousness of saints. And he saith unto me, Write,

> Blessed are they which are called unto the marriage supper of the Lamb.
>
> —Revelation 19:6–9 KJV

What will Christ say in that moment? While we won't know for sure until we are there, perhaps the song "Beloved" will capture it well:

> Love of my life
> Look deep in my eyes
> There you will find what you need
> I'm the giver of life
> I'll clothe you in white
> My immaculate bride you will be
> Oh come running home to me
>
> You're my beloved
> Lover I'm yours
> Death shall not part us
> It's you I died for
> For better or worse
> Forever we'll be
> Our Love it unites us
> It binds you to me
> It's a mystery[53]

The love that Christ, the bridegroom, has for us—believers, His bride—is perhaps the deepest and greatest mystery in the Bible. While we can never hope to understand it, we can rejoice in the fact that He has prepared a beautiful place for us and that we will be able to experience the wonders of that love for eternity. As Jesus said to His disciples while He was on earth, "If I go and prepare a place for you, I will come again, and receive you unto myself; that where I am, there ye may be also" (John 14:3 KJV).

It is a promise we can look forward to, and a love we can enjoy every day.

APPENDIX

VERSES ON MARRIAGE, HUSBANDS, AND WIVES

Ephesians 5:22–33

Wives, submit to your own husbands, as to the Lord. For the husband is head of the wife, as also Christ is head of the church; and He is the Savior of the body. Therefore, just as the church is subject to Christ, so let the wives be to their own husbands in everything. Husbands, love your wives, just as Christ also loved the church and gave Himself for her, that He might sanctify and cleanse her with the washing of water by the word, that He might present her to Himself a glorious church, not having spot or wrinkle or any such thing, but that she should be holy and without blemish. So husbands ought to love their own wives as their own bodies; he who loves his wife loves himself. For no one ever hated his own flesh, but nourishes and cherishes it, just as the Lord does the church. For we are members of His body, of His flesh and of His bones. "For this reason a man shall leave his father and mother and be joined to his wife, and the two shall become one flesh." This is a great mystery, but I speak concerning Christ and the church. Nevertheless let each one of you in particular so love his own wife as himself, and let the wife see that she respects her husband.

Colossians 3:18–19

Wives, submit to your own husbands, as is fitting in the Lord. Husbands, love your wives and do not be bitter toward them.

1 Peter 3:1–9

Wives, likewise, be submissive to your own husbands, that even if some do not obey the word, they, without a word, may be won by the conduct of their wives, when they observe your chaste conduct accompanied by fear. Do not let your adornment be merely outward—arranging the hair, wearing gold, or putting on fine apparel—rather let it be the hidden person of the heart, with the incorruptible beauty of a gentle and quiet spirit, which is very precious in the sight of God. For in this manner, in former times, the holy women who trusted in God also adorned themselves, being submissive to their own husbands, as Sarah obeyed Abraham, calling him lord, whose daughters you are if you do good and are not afraid with any terror. Husbands, likewise, dwell with them with understanding, giving honor to the wife, as to the weaker vessel, and as being heirs together of the grace of life, that your prayers may not be hindered. Finally, all of you be of one mind, having compassion for one another; love as brothers, be tenderhearted, be courteous; not returning evil for evil or reviling for reviling, but on the contrary blessing, knowing that you were called to this, that you may inherit a blessing.

BIBLIOGRAPHY

Aliz, Imtiaz (director) and Saif Ali Khan (producer). *Love Aaj Kal*. India: Illuminati Films in association with Eros International, 2009. http://www.boxofficeindia.com/showProd.php?itemCat=290&catName=MjAwOQ==

Barna, George. *Unmarried America*. Glendale, CA: Barna Research Group, Ltd., 1993. Cited in Dennis Franck, "Single Adults—A Population Group Too Large to Ignore," Enrichment Journal. http://enrichmentjournal.ag.org/200003/030_too_large.cfm

Barry, Dave. "She Drives for a Relationship; He's Lost in the Transmission." *Dave Barry's Complete Guide to Guys*. New York: Ballantine Books, 1996. http://homepage.eircom.net/~odyssey/Quotes/Modern_World/Dbr.html.

Beam, Joe. "Do I Have a Soul Mate?" Marriage Helper 911, Beam Research Center, January 28, 2011. http://www.marriagehelper.com/soul_mate.php

Chelsom, Peter (director), Simon Fields, Peter Abrams, and Robert L. Levy (producers). *Serendipity*. United States: Miramax Films, 2001.

"Divorce Rate Lowest for 29 Years." BBC News, January 28, 2010. http://news.bbc.co.uk/2/hi/uk_news/8485132.stm

Encyclopedia Britannica. "Romanticism." Encyclopedia Britannica Inc., 2003. http://www.britannica.com/EBchecked/topic/ 508675/Romanticism

"Family of Modesto Teacher Who Moved in with Student Needs 'Space.'" *L.A. Now*, March 5, 2012. http://latimesblogs.latimes.com/lanow/2012/03/modesto-teacher-left-family-james-hooker.html

"Four in 10 First Marriages End in Divorce: Report." CBC News, October 4, 2010. http://www.cbc.ca/news/canada/story/2010/10/04/vanier-study004.html

Gardner, Tim Alan. "Secrets of a Soul Mate," *Today's Christian Woman,* September 2008. http://www.todayschristianwoman.com/articles/2008/september/secrets-of-soul-mate.html

Gessle, Per. "It Must Have Been Love." Recorded by Roxette on the album *Christmas for the Broken Hearted.* Germany: EMI, 1987.

Green, Michael (editor). "Feeling, Faith and Fact," quoted in *Bible Illustrations for Preaching.* Grand Rapids, MI: Baker Books, 1989.

Larsen, Jo Ann. "A Most Extraordinary Event," *Deseret News,* 1992. http://www.christianity.com/devotionals/devotions-for-married-couples/dr-dobsons-married-couples-devotional-jan-1.html

Lewis, C.S. *The Four Loves*. New York: Harcourt Brace, 1960.

Lowman, Pete. *A Long Way East of Eden*. United States: Paternoster. Milton Keynes, UK: Paternoster Publishing, 2002. http://www.bethinking.org/culture-worldview/

intermediate/a-long-way-east-of-eden-5-love-after-god.htm

Mann, Barry, Phil Spector, and Cynthia Weil. "You've Lost That Lovin' Feeling." Recorded by The Righteous Brothers on the album *You've Lost That Lovin' Feeling*. United States: Philles, 1964.

Marx, Richard. "This I Promise You," recorded by 'N Sync on *No Strings Attached*. United States: Jive Records, 2000.

"Marriages and Divorces, Australia, 2010." Australian Bureau of Statistics, November 30, 2011. http://www.abs.gov.au/ausstats/abs@.nsf/mf/3310.0

"Modesto Teacher Resigns, Moves in with 18-year-old Student." *L.A. Now*, February 29, 2012. http://latimesblogs.latimes.com/lanow/2012/02/california-teacher-resigns-moves-in-with-18-year-old-student.html

"New Report Sheds Light on Trends and Patterns in Marriage, Divorce, and Cohabitation." Centers for Disease Control and Prevention, July 23, 2002. http://www.cdc.gov/media/pressrel/r020724.htm

Peck, Scott M. *The Road Less Traveled*. New York: Simon and Schuster, 1978.

Qu, Lixia and Ruth Weston. "Trends in Couple Dissolution: An Update." Australian Institute of Family Studies, *Family Relationships Quarterly No. 19*, March 29, 2012. http://www.aifs.gov.au/afrc/pubs/newsletter/frq019/frq019-4.html

Rogers, Simon. "For Richer, but Not Poorer: Recession Blamed for Rise in Divorce Rates." *The Guardian*, December 8, 2011. http://www.guardian.co.uk/lifeandstyle/2011/dec/08/richer-poorer-recession-divorce-rates

Sherbert, Erin. "James Hooker, Modesto Teacher Who Ditched Wife and Kids for Student, Should Lose His Pension, Lawmaker Says." *San Francisco Weekly*, March

15, 2012. http://blogs.sfweekly.com/thesnitch/2012/03/james_hooker_modesto_teacher_w.php

Sheriden, Kirsten (director) and Richard Barton Lewis (producer). *August Rush.* United States: Warner Bros., 2007.

Shugerman, Lindsay. "Percentage of Married Couples Who Cheat," Catalogs.com Info Library. http://www.catalogs.com/info/relationships/percentage-of-married-couples-who-cheat-on-each-ot.html

Silberling, Brad (director), Charles Roven and Dawn Steel (producers). *City of Angels.* United States: Warner Bros., 1998.

Temke, Mary W. "The Effects of Divorce on Children." University of New Hampshire. extension.unh.edu/Family/Documents/divorce.pdf

Tennov, Dorothy. "Characteristics of Limerence—A Brief Description by Dr. Tennov," *The Collected Works of Dorothy Tennov.* http://www.scribd.com/doc/112511817/DTCW-02-Desc-Glos-Comm

Tenth Avenue North. "Beloved," from the album *Over and Underneath.* Brentwood, TN: Reunion, 2008.

"Top 10 Romantic Movies." KidzWorld, 2012. http://www.kidz-world.com/article/22971-top-10-romantic-movies-2010

Disney, Walt. *Snow White and the Seven Dwarfs.* United States: Walt Disney Productions, 1937.

——. *Sleeping Beauty.* United States: Walt Disney Productions, 1959.

——. *Pocahontas.* United States: Walt Disney Pictures, 1995.

Ward, Vincent (director). *What Dreams May Come* (motion picture). United States: PolyGram Film/Universal Pictures, 1998.

Warren, Diane. "I Want You to Need Me." Recorded by Celine Dion on the album *All the Way ... A Decade of Song.* Paradise Studios: Columbia Epic, 2000.

Youngblood, Richard F. (editor). *Nelson's Student Bible Dictionary.* Nashville, TN: Thomas Nelson, 1986.

ENDNOTES

Chapter 1: Snow White Said So

1. *Snow White and the Seven Dwarfs,* Walt Disney Productions, 1938.
2. As of 2011, with the most recent being *Winnie the Pooh.*
3. *Sleeping Beauty,* Walt Disney Productions, 1959.
4. *Pocahontas,* Walt Disney Productions, 1995.
5. "Top 10 Romantic Movies," KidzWorld, 2012. http://www.kidzworld.com/article/22971-top-10-romantic-movies-2010.
6. Diane Warren, "I Want You to Need Me." Recorded by Celine Dion on the album *All the Way . . . A Decade of Song.* Paradise Studios: Columbia Epic, 2000.
7. Imtiaz Ali (director) and Saif Ali Khan (producer), *Love Aaj Kal.* India: Illuminati Films in association with Eros International, 2009. http://www.boxofficeindia.com/showProd.php?itemCat=290&catName=MjAwOQ==
8. *Encyclopedia Britannica,* "Romanticism." http://www.britannica.com/EBchecked/topic/508675/Romanticism.

9. C.S. Lewis, *The Four Loves* (New York: Harcourt, Brace, 1960), 93.
10. Richard Marx, "This I Promise You," recorded by 'N Sync on *No Strings Attached* (Jive Records, 2000).

Chapter 2: The Soul-Mate Deception

11. Vincent Ward (director), Stephen Deutsh and Barnet Bain (producers), *What Dreams May Come*. United States: PolyGram Film/Universal Pictures, 1998.

Chapter 3: The Real World

12. "New Report Sheds Light on Trends and Patterns in Marriage, Divorce, and Cohabitation," Centers for Disease Control and Prevention, July 23, 2002. http://www.cdc.gov/media/pressrel/r020724.htm
13. Lixia Qu and Ruth Weston, "Trends in Couple Dissolution: An Update," Australian Institute of Family Studies, *Family Relationships Quarterly No. 19*, March 29, 2012. http://www.aifs.gov.au/afrc/pubs/newsletter/frq019/frq019-4.html
14. Unless otherwise noted, the statistics in this chapter are taken from http://www.divorcerate.org/
15. George Barna, *Unmarried America* (Glendale, CA: Barna Research Group, Ltd., 1993), 22. Cited in Dennis Franck, "Single Adults—A Population Group Too Large to Ignore," Enrichment Journal. http://enrichmentjournal.ag.org/200003/030_too_large.cfm
16. "Four in 10 First Marriages End in Divorce: Report," CBC News, October 4, 2010. http://www.cbc.ca/news/canada/story/2010/10/04/vanier-study004.html
17. Simon Rogers. "For Richer, but Not Poorer: Recession Blamed for Rise in Divorce Rates," *The Guardian*, December

8, 2011. http://www.guardian.co.uk/lifeandstyle/2011/dec/08/richer-poorer-recession-divorce-rates

18. "Divorce Rate Lowest for 29 Years," BBC News, January 28, 2010. http://news.bbc.co.uk/2/hi/uk_news/8485132.stm
19. "Marriages and Divorces, Australia, 2010," Australian Bureau of Statistics, November 30, 2011. http://www.abs.gov.au/ausstats/abs@.nsf/mf/3310.0
20. Pete Lowman, *A Long Way East of Eden* (Milton Keynes, UK: Paternoster Publishing, 2002), http://www.bethinking.org/culture-worldview/intermediate/a-long-way-east-of-eden-5-love-after-god.htm
21. Mary W. Temke, "The Effects of Divorce on Children," University of New Hampshire. extension.unh.edu/Family/Documents/divorce.pdf
22. "Family of Modesto Teacher Who Moved in with Student Needs 'Space,'" *L.A. Now*, March 5, 2012. http://latimesblogs.latimes.com/lanow/2012/03/modesto-teacher-left-family-james-hooker.html
23. "Modesto Teacher Resigns, Moves in with 18-year-old Student," *L.A. Now*, February 29, 2012. http://latimesblogs.latimes.com/lanow/2012/02/california-teacher-resigns-moves-in-with-18-year-old-student.html
24. C.S. Lewis, *The Four Loves* (New York: Harcourt, 1960), 159, 161.
25. Erin Sherbert, "James Hooker, Modesto Teacher Who Ditched Wife and Kids for Student, Should Lose His Pension, Lawmaker Says," *San Francisco Weekly*, March 15, 2012. http://blogs.sfweekly.com/thesnitch/2012/03/james_hooker_modesto_teacher_w.php

Chapter 4: Love or Limerence?

26. Per Gessle, "It Must Have Been Love," recorded by Roxette on the album *Christmas for the Broken Hearted* (Germany: EMI, 1987).
27. Dorothy Tennov, "Characteristics of Limerence—A Brief Description by Dr. Tennov," *The Collected Works of Dorothy Tennov.* http://www.scribd.com/doc/112511817/DTCW-02-Desc-Glos-Comm
28. Joe Beam, "Do I Have a Soul Mate?" Marriage Helper 911, Beam Research Center, January 28, 2011. http://www.marriagehelper.com/soul_mate.php
29. Ibid.
30. Tennov, "Characteristics of Limerence—A Brief Description by Dr. Tennov."
31. Scott M. Peck, *The Road Less Traveled* (New York: Simon and Schuster, 1978), 84–85.
32. Tennov, "Characteristics of Limerence—A Brief Description by Dr. Tennov."
33. Beam, "Do I Have a Soul Mate?"

Chapter 5: *Agape* and Other Greek Words

34. C.S. Lewis, *The Four Loves* (New York: Harcourt, Brace, 1960), 21–22.
35. Ibid., 162
36. Ibid., 164.
37. Ibid., 61.
38. Ibid., 130.
39. Ibid., 171.
40. Ibid., 174.

Chapter 6: The Battle between Faith and Feelings

41. "Feeling, Faith and Fact," quoted in Michael Green, editor, *Bible Illustrations for Preaching* (Grand Rapids, MI: Baker Books, 1989).

Chapter 7: A True Foundation

42. Richard F. Youngblood, editor, *Nelson's Student Bible Dictionary* (Nashville, TN: Thomas Nelson, 1986).
43. Ibid.

Chapter 8: Till Death Do Us Part

44. C.S. Lewis, *The Four Loves* (New York: Harcourt, Brace, 1960), 170.

Chapter 10: He Said, She Said

45. Adapted from Dave Barry, "She Drives for a Relationship; He's Lost in the Transmission," *Dave Barry's Complete Guide to Guys* (New York: Ballantine Books, 1996).

Chapter 11: Lost That Lovin' Feeling?

46. Barry Mann, Phil Spector, and Cynthia Weil, "You've Lost That Lovin' Feeling," recorded by The Righteous Brothers on the album *You've Lost That Lovin' Feeling* (United States: Philles, 1964).
47. Tim Alan Gardner, "Secrets of a Soul Mate," *Today's Christian Woman,* September 2008. http://www.todayschristianwoman.com/articles/2008/september/secrets-of-soul-mate.html
48. Ibid.

Chapter 12: Time for a Tune-Up

49. Jo Ann Larsen, "A Most Extraordinary Event," *Deseret News,* 1992.?? Do you mean Deseret? YES! http://www.christianity.com/devotionals/devotions-for-married-couples/dr-dobsons-married-couples-devotional-jan-1.html

Chapter 13: Beyond Repair?

50. Lindsay Shugerman, "Percentage of Married Couples Who Cheat," Catalogs.com Info Library. http://www.catalogs.com/info/relationships/percentage-of-married-couples-who-cheat-on-each-ot.html
51. Note that forgiveness can be a bit tricky, as it is not the same thing as naïveté or allowing oneself to remain in a dangerous situation. Many people who refuse to leave abusive or negative codependent relationships use forgiveness as the reason. This section on forgiveness is not intended to be used as an encouragement to stay in a negative, hurtful, or abusive relationship.
52. Bethinking.org - Culture + Worldview - A Long Way East of … (n.d.). Retrieved from http://www.bethinking.org/culture-worldview/intermediate/a-long-way-east-of-eden-5-love-after-god.htm

Epilogue

53. Tenth Avenue North, "Beloved," from the album *Over and Underneath* (Brentwood, TN: Reunion, 2008).

CPSIA information can be obtained at www.ICGtesting.com
Printed in the USA
LVOW11s0839051213

363899LV00003B/41/P